Praise

'This book gives entrepreneurs the fast track to becoming really successful. It's full of great insights and wisdom on how owning a solid franchise could be your unfair advantage in business.'
— **Ash Ali**, Award winning author of
The Unfair Advantage

'If you are looking for consolidated knowledge about business mastery, this is the book to read. Rune's 20+ years of franchising, marketing and business makes this book the ABC for any entrepreneur.'
— **Dani Peleva**, Founder and CEO
Franchise Fame

'In his business, Rune has already proved himself to be an exceptional entrepreneur. Now, he reveals the secrets to his success and the lessons he has learned through franchising Fantastic Services. If you are thinking of franchising, be sure to read this book.'
— **Carl Reader**, bestselling author

'Mastering a business with the intricate art of franchising is something very few authors have captured as well as Rune. It is simply a must read for any current or prospective franchisor and growth business.'
— **Sean Goldsmith**, Groe Global

'As the architect of one of the most dynamic franchised businesses of the past decade, Rune Sovndahl's advice, knowledge and experience is second to none. So, this book is absolutely the one to read if you're serious about successfully franchising a business.'

    – **Clive Smith**, Franchise Focus

'The principles that Fantastic Business has outlined will help any entrepreneur, no matter how big or small the company is. These lessons can be applied to startups as well because they are not only focused on franchises but also encompass all aspects of running any successful business.'

    – **Erik Van Horn**, Franchise Secrets

FANTASTIC BUSINESS

Start, scale and
succeed, learning from
masters in franchising

**RUNE
SOVNDAHL**

R^ethink

First published in Great Britain in 2022 by Rethink Press (www.rethinkpress.com)

For all of Us

We have the opportunity to take action and
accountability for our planet now

Contents

Introduction

Business is essentially about solving a problem and serving a greater purpose, in a profitable way.

The problem I saw back in 2008 was that when booking a carpet cleaning service online, it was impossible to see the price and availability of that service. Potential customers had to contact the service provider directly, and this was inefficient. Often the phone wasn't answered or the contact details were wrong, which led to lost business and unhappy customers. And this wasn't just the case for cleaning services but all types of domestic services, from carpet cleaning to pest control and waste removal.

Seeing the problem, we created a start-up that would fix it, and it was the process of starting, scaling and succeeding in that business that taught me the fundamental, evergreen principles I'll share with you in this book. Each chapter will offer something that's relevant to where you are in your business, whether you're just starting out or have been running it for a decade or more. My aim with this book is to help anyone who's in business, no matter what type or size it might be.

I started my entrepreneurial journey after my first job in 2000, and I've run a number of start-ups since, some successful and some not so successful. My background is in the interaction between humans and computers. My businesses have included music schools, telecoms and online marketing agencies, as well as online operations for smaller companies. Through all of them, I've learned that the most important thing when it comes to success is serving and understanding the customer; make the business operationally efficient and that growth is about creating better-performing teams.

I've also learned that the success of a project isn't due to the technology that's being used but to how you apply it. In this book, I'm going to show you exactly what I mean.

I started Fantastic Services in 2009, just as the credit crisis recession started. Few businesses survive a decade and even fewer survive and thrive through three crises – the 2009 banking crisis, Brexit and the 2020 pandemic crisis. But Fantastic Services has reinvented itself time and time again and continues to grow, despite the enormous pressures it has faced, and it will continue to, no matter what comes next.

This level of success is rare for any company, let alone a company that was started with less than £3,000 in investment. I'm proud that Fantastic Services is one of the few bootstrapped companies in the multi-million-pound category.

We've seen off start-ups that raised multi-million-pound funds and then spent all the money on marketing and technology, yet didn't get close to the customer or growth. Throughout the history of Fantastic Services, we've always had to make it work with what we've had. A sense of urgency like this teaches you skills. It's often said, 'If at first you don't succeed, change and adapt.' Every problem is a chance of a new solution and the principles in this book are based on this philosophy. This is a book about fast-paced sustainable growth and lasting efforts. Bad companies fail in a crisis. Good companies survive. Great companies become truly fantastic. This book will teach you how to make your business fantastic.

When we started Fantastic Services, we didn't immediately think of franchising but soon saw that there's something inherently beautiful about it. Franchising is about a local business, investing locally and employing local people. It gives ownership and control to the people running it. The values of the franchisee are important. We chose this business model because business owners never get the level of support they need from the open marketplace. Franchising is the only business model in which peer support, mentoring and training are built into the very fabric of the business – it's all about shared ownership.

That said, the principles in this book will help you whether you're a franchisor, a franchisee or an entrepreneur. At Fantastic Services we started out with six vans, and now we've got over 450 vans in London alone, branches all over the world, and we continue to grow. There's no reason why you can't enjoy similar success.

For this book, I interviewed more than twenty-five CEOs of franchises and more than 100 franchisees. Not all case studies are included, but the important principles and the best examples remain so we can learn about marketing, sales, training and the importance of repetition. In business there will be times when you're refreshing and repeating and there will be times when you're optimising and maximising. These are phases that I've gone through with Fantastic Services in over a decade and a half of business. I know what works and what doesn't. Ultimately, being successful in business means uncovering the essence of why we do what we do and making sure that we stay true to our purpose. It's this that will carry you through when times are hard.

Success isn't measured by your enterprise value or your share price but by how well you've been able to weather the storm and make a lasting impact in a constantly changing world. It's about how well you have passed the planet on to future generations – after all, a business isn't about its leader, but about every single person within the company, and the legacy you leave for future generations. Making a 360-degree circle of happiness with our stakeholders, the owners, the staff the professionals, our partners and the planet, is something we have adapted from the start.

At Fantastic Services we still treat every day as if it's a new day and a new company, and I hope this book helps you to do the same with your business.

ONE

The Power Of Togetherness

Franchising is a partnership. It's all about the power of togetherness. It's about having a common goal and peers to help you in your growth and development. A franchise is a business in a box that takes you outside the box.

The great thing about franchises is that both parties benefit from the business model. The franchisor benefits because they're able to expand their business rapidly without having to invest heavily in financing, and the franchisee benefits because they're able to own a business without any of the risks involved with founding a start-up.

McDonalds and Domino's are among the best-known franchise businesses, but the franchise business model doesn't just work for fast-food restaurants. Driving schools, cleaning companies, baby classes and many other types of businesses also run successfully on a franchise model.

I'm a fan of franchising because, put simply, a franchise is a business that has been predefined. The business model has been tried and tested, so you know it works. A franchise comes with a history of how to run it, and its founders understand the key success factors in the business and the processes required to make it successful.

For individuals, a franchise offers a great way to start running your own business without having to start from scratch. Not only do you have the reassurance of a proven business plan, products and/or services, you've also got the backing of a team of highly experienced people who can help you achieve your business goals. For this reason, franchises can have a much higher success rate than start-ups. For example, 80% of start-ups fail within five years, whereas in the same period, 80% of franchises succeed.[1] According to 2019 research based on official census data, the two-year franchise

---

1. Lafontaine, F, Zapletal, M, and Zhang, X, 'Brighter prospects? Assessing the franchise advantage using census data', *Journal of Economics & Management Strategy*, 28/2 (5 October 2018), https://onlinelibrary.wiley.com/doi/10.1111/jems.12289, accessed 27 April 2022

success rate is about 8% higher than the independent business success rate. The one-year survival rate for franchises is about 6.3% higher.[2]

A franchise is also much more than simply a business. It's a relationship and a partnership where the franchisor's skills are synergised with the franchisee's skills. Both parties grow as the business grows. In my opinion, a franchise business is one of the strongest and longest-lasting business models there is, and I'll explain why in this book. We'll also examine the principles behind starting, scaling and enjoying a fantastic franchise business.

What makes a great franchise?

Some people see a franchise as something to sell upfront – the franchise itself is where the profit comes from. But the moment you say you're selling a franchise, you're doing it wrong.

Instead, think of it as granting a licence to use your brand and access the training and systems. A franchise is an investment. The master fee or the initial fee shouldn't make up the franchisor's income – there

---

2. Lafontaine, F, Zapletal, M, and Zhang, X, 'Brighter prospects? Assessing the franchise advantage using census data', *Journal of Economics & Management Strategy*, 28/2 (5 October 2018), https://onlinelibrary.wiley.com/doi/10.1111/jems.12289, accessed 27 April 2022

should be an ongoing steady revenue stream. The only way to achieve a sustainable long-term business is to make sure that royalties feed the company, not the initial fee that the franchisee pays.

In fact, one of the key differences between a successful franchise and a successful **long-term** franchise is the way in which income is earned. A lot of companies can go out and sell 500 franchises, but only half of those will be operational after a year, and after ten years, many may not operate very well. To be successful, franchises need to be partnerships where revenue growth is supported long-term, enabling the franchisee to build their own business while also supporting the franchise itself.

This is why a franchise has to be a partnership. Of course, the franchisee has to follow brand guidelines and certain rules, but ultimately they're in business *for themselves*, not *by themselves*.

Many small rivers run into an ocean

A good franchise is one whose owners really understand the business. They know that they're stronger with their franchisees than without, and they see the importance of running a business as a partnership. They appreciate the importance of ownership and accountability, and work to ensure that all their franchisees are supported and encouraged to grow in line with their own ambitions.

Turning a good franchise into a *great* franchise requires the recognition that the franchise business model is a partnership, meaning many small rivers turn into an ocean. A great franchise has the right technology, processes, systems and, most importantly, people in place to get the best not only out of the franchisees, but also out of the franchisor.

I know from talking to hundreds of franchisees that some don't understand everything about the operating model and others aren't the best at systems or marketing, but a great franchisor will be there to help them with the things they find challenging. As a result, the franchisee becomes more confident and more successful, meaning both parties become better, more scalable and generate more revenue.

Who are franchisees?

Most franchisees either have a little bit of cash that they want to invest, are looking for a career change, or have decided to move into a new location. A lot of franchisees have been managers before but are often not the typical nine-to-five sort of person. They come from both blue- and white-collar backgrounds. What they have in common is that they want to work *for* themselves but not *by* themselves.

Many people have the desire to work for themselves but feel they aren't ready for the full responsibility of doing so. They don't know what to do, how to set up and operate a business. This is why franchising proves so popular – it marries ambition with know-how and support. We like to think of the franchise model as making ambitions come true.

Founding a business takes an enormous amount of work, time and risk. You need to find the right product or service to sell, decide on pricing and work out your branding and marketing strategy while also trying to figure out the systems you need to put in place to get the operations right, to get the legal considerations right, etc. The list is endless and it can be daunting when it's all new to you.

With a franchise, you can skip 90% of the steps involved in founding a business because it's all been done for you. You know the product or service and the price you need to sell it at. The branding, the uniforms, the equipment, the vehicles, the software – everything you need has been sourced for you. Basically, a franchise gives you a head start.

Franchisees vs entrepreneurs

Franchisees could be described as novice entrepreneurs. They have the desire and ambition, but not necessarily the capabilities. In the business world, there's a view that franchisees aren't entrepreneurs, and there's a kind of snobbery about it. But I can tell you that franchisees are very much entrepreneurs. Entrepreneurs are people who invest in others, or in themselves, to create a business opportunity. It's about finding an area and then committing to it and investing in it. So being an entrepreneur is about taking a chance that a salaried person, or a worker, doesn't take. Entrepreneurs step up and stand on their own two feet.

If you're investing in a business, then you're an entrepreneur. Simple.

There is most definitely a difference between being a franchisee and creating a start-up, though. The latter is like running fast down a runway before a big cliff edge to take off and trying to assemble an airplane before you crash or manage to take off. With franchising, you're still taking off on the runway, but the airplane is already assembled, you have the manuals, the guide and have been shown how the controls work, and where to go. That's a big difference in risk. Both are entrepreneurs – they're jumping off the same runway – but franchisees have the support to make a success of their journey from the moment they set off, making everything much less scary.

The unknown success of the franchisee

The media bombards us with stories of billion-dollar start-ups and twenty-five-year-old entrepreneurs who've sold their businesses for millions, but we rarely hear about the millionaire franchisees. The story of the multi-unit franchisees who really make it is often not told. They also don't have to tell their stories – they just have to enjoy the success.

I know a franchisee who owns seven of our franchises. He moved to South America from Europe and lives a good life. He has people managing his franchise businesses and is able to live the life he wants having grown his businesses successfully. He's got the champagne lifestyle without having had to invent anything or come up with a business of his own. He simply had to invest and follow the pathway that was set out for him.

The little-known thing about franchises is that once you have one and learn how to run it successfully, it's easier to scale or replicate your success and compound it. The most successful franchisees own multiple franchises. Franchising allows you to create a business empire without the challenge of having to build it alone.

Multi-entrepreneur Elon Musk talks about how hard it is to be responsible for everything all the time.[3] With a franchise, the only thing that you're responsible for is yourself. You're only accountable to the franchisor or staff, so there's a different level of responsibility. Sure, you have to manage the business, and you're responsible for the parts that you manage, but ultimately,

3. Zoldan, A, 'This weird advice from Elon Musk is a must-read for every budding entrepreneur', *Inc.* (23 October 2017) www.inc.com /ari-zoldan/this-weird-advice-from-elon-musk-is-a-must-read-for -every-budding-entrepreneur.html, accessed 27 April 2022

you don't have the same challenges as an owner of a start-up.

As a franchisee you also have more choices. You can choose the lifestyle that you want early on in the journey. You can even move to a different country and manage the franchise from there – an 'absentee franchisee'. This often isn't the case when you build a start-up. The Queen of England is actually an example of an absentee franchisee[4]. The Crown Estate owns a McDonald's and a couple of other franchise businesses but has probably never set foot in one. The franchise business can be managed from afar or managed for you by your managers.

Franchises are an investment, and they can be businesses that run themselves and generate profit. Owning one offers you a low-risk, high-reward way of being an entrepreneur. With franchises, it's possible to make your money work for you and not the other way around, and it's this that makes them fantastic.

Fantastic Services

When we started Fantastic Services, we saw that with the right training and the right systems and processes in place within a business, people could easily go

---

4.   Walansky, A, 'Queen Elizabeth owns a McDonald's that serves tea and porridge', *Today* (25 October 2017), www.today.com/food/queen -elizabeth-owns-mcdonald-s-uk-t117963, accessed 27 April 2022

from, for example, operating a single carpet cleaning van to owning five of them, and then to owning four carpet cleaning companies, a removal business and a pest-control business.

It didn't matter what background these people had or what their experience was – they could become successful if they were supported. We realised that by creating opportunities and supplementing these with robust support systems, we'd make it easier for all franchisees to scale and be successful.

Again, with a franchising system, if you know what you're doing, you can replicate your success over and over and become more successful than you ever thought possible. I've seen it happen many times.

TOP TIPS FOR FRANCHISING

1. **Work out how much you can invest.** Banks tend to be favourable to franchisees and backing can be easier to get; having developed relationships with many banks, it's easy to see why, because the franchisee come with business plans, and they're proven entities. The longer the franchise has been running, the easier it is to get funding. Every single franchisee is a case study of success, and this is what the banks are looking for. You might be surprised by how much easier it is to borrow money to start a franchise than it is to find investment for a start-up (due to the much lower risk profile of a franchised business).

How much you invest will of course depend on your personal circumstances. Some franchises require you to invest in premises, vehicles and equipment, and there's a range of investment options out there. A working franchise is by far the cheapest option. The only thing you'll need to invest in is a piece of equipment, and you can start working straight away.

If you invest in a master franchise, you'll probably have to invest in more than one type of equipment, or you might have to buy or lease five or six vans, or five or six carpet cleaning machines. You're also going to have to invest in more marketing. An area franchise requires less investment in equipment, but more selling skills, and for a country franchise you'll need to pay a licensing fee and also make larger investments in marketing. The thing to remember is that there's a franchise model to suit everyone's circumstances, and they'll all be looked upon favourably by the banks.

2. **Choose your partner.** Get to know the franchise. You're not just buying a 'business in a box'. What you're buying is a long-term commitment to growing a business, and it's only by meeting with franchisees and interviewing the franchisor that you'll understand what type of business is best suited to you. It's critical to do your research and find the business that's going to be the best fit.

3. **Know how much support you'll receive.** Not everyone is made for self-study. For a lot of people, being given an operations manual and told to get on with it isn't going to be helpful. It's important that you look into the support that will be available to you. Know how much help you'll receive once you take the franchise on. The best franchisors provide

training and ongoing support and will be a true partner as you start your business journey, and in some cases some services are provided at reduced cost by teams at central headquarters. You get the benefit of large corporations but at affordable prices.

4. **Find a franchise that suits your interests or experiences.** It might sound obvious, but the key to running a successful franchise is finding one that matches your skills and interests. If you're in a service business, for example, it's important that you have good communication skills and can manage and motivate people effectively. If you don't like managing and recruiting people, or can't find a partner or operations manager who can, then a service business is probably not for you, but there are plenty of other options to explore.

5. **Follow your joy.** You don't want to monetise your passions, as we will go into in Chapter 7, but it's important that you have goals to achieve and are passionate about what you do. It might be that you're passionate about providing for your family, achieving a particular lifestyle or running a business with a good ethos. Regardless, you always need to be looking ahead, and you should have an idea of where you want to end up.

Summary

In this chapter, I've introduced the concept of the franchise and why it makes good business sense to take one on. Being a franchisee is the safe way to become an entrepreneur, and if you take on board the tips for franchising, you have every chance of being successful.

In the next chapter, I'll explain how to get started.

TWO

Mastering Franchises

In the first chapter, we defined a franchise as a proven profitable partnership. In this chapter, we're going to go deeper into how franchising works and what makes the business model so successful.

Start with your mindset

The most important thing to do to become a successful franchisee is to master your mindset.

You have to adopt a growth mindset. When starting a franchise, it's vital to ask for help and listen to other people. When you have a growth mindset, you're not too proud to ask for the help you need, and you'll find that when you're open to learning and willing to listen, you'll create great partnerships. When you focus on understanding what it is you need to do with the mindset of 'I just have to do this', I am accountable, I'm the person who will make this a success, when you accept your responsibility and take action, you'll be successful.

Another great thing about franchise businesses is that because you're following a tried and tested way of doing things, you'll be advised about the order you need to do things in and the best way to do them.

For example, when you start out with a new franchise, you'll need to upgrade your LinkedIn profile, start doing outreach, make specific types of sales, invest in flyers and marketing etc. There's a lot involved, but there's also a proven strategy to follow. You'll be provided with the resources you need, and if you have a growth mindset you'll learn a lot from the process.

Remember that you're investing

You're not *buying* a franchise – you're *investing* in a franchise. Go in with this mindset. When you invest in a franchise, you're investing in an asset. That asset can be resold, and it can be resold for more when it's successful.

RED Driving School is a good example of a franchise that knows exactly what to invest in and when. Ian McIntosh, the CEO of RED Driving School, invests heavily in training drivers and delivering quality. The result is that RED like Fantastic Services achieves four-star plus reviews on Trustpilot, and Google.

Successful businesses have more than just good products. RED Driving School, just as we do in Fantastic Services, goes deep on the training, and the quality of the delivery means that they're always going to get those great reviews. Ultimately, great reviews mean new customers and brand recognition. It's well known that if you have a bad experience, you'll likely tell ten people and if you have an incredible experience you'll only tell two or three. As a business owner you've got to do everything you can to capitalise on the good reviews.

Why franchising makes good business sense

Franchises vs start-ups

As discussed, with franchising, you're not building a business from scratch. Yes, you have to buy certain equipment and spend time and money getting everything together, but you don't have to spend a year or more of trial and error to find out what works best. You're starting with what's best.

You're taking an existing model that already works and growing it in a way that works for you. The key to being a successful franchisee is to learn from others and replicate the things that they've done successfully.

When you're starting up a business on your own, you have to develop everything yourself, from the name and product market fit to pricing strategy, target market, branding and email templates. You have to build your social media presence and figure out how to manage and motivate your staff. You'll also need a website or an app, you'll need to choose a software system, you'll need to find out how to receive payment online and determine how and when to recruit and also what to put in your adverts. There's a lot to get your head around, and it's not an easy task. It really is about assembling an airplane while jumping off a cliff.

On top of that, you have to secure funding. And because you don't have any proof that your system will work, you don't have a success story to share and it will be harder to get funding. Growing a start-up can be immensely fun and satisfying if you're a creative and like to tinker, but it can also be a complete waste of time if you keep going in the wrong direction. That's why franchising makes so much sense.

Investing in a franchise doesn't exempt you from the hard work that's involved in getting a business off the ground, but it definitely saves you from the admin.

If it's a successful franchise business with many franchises within it, such as Fantastic Services, it will have failed many times and learned from those failures. These lessons will have been passed on to the franchisees. The research will have been done. All you'll need to do is hit the 'go' button.

Franchising vs property

Property usually grows in value, which makes it a good asset. Eventually, you'll likely see a return on the money you put in. Owning a franchise requires more work than owning a property, but you also get a much quicker, and often bigger, return on your investment.

A franchise allows you to build income while working and can have enormous cash rewards. There may be times when you're not making much profit, but it can still give you that freedom and quality of life you'll never have as a paid employee in somebody else's business. You need to have energy and drive, though. Franchising isn't for lazy people who simply want a passive income. There is no overnight success with franchising.

When you invest in a franchise, you can achieve a good standard of living and grow an asset that will always increase in value. Franchising also lets you diversify your portfolio in the same way that you might invest in a diverse portfolio of properties. In fact, if you already have a good property portfolio, an area franchise model will make a good addition to your property portfolio.

You can access the franchise businesses that provide property maintenance services and grow both businesses together if you're smart about it.

Franchising vs shares

Shares are an investment over which you have little control. Investing in shares is passive, whereas franchising is active. For most franchisees, including me, investing in shares isn't a satisfying way to invest. This is because franchisees are driven, high-energy people who want to do something with their money that's more active. If you want an exciting way to grow your money, investing in shares won't give you that return on your energy.

The flexibility of a franchise

I don't necessarily recommend having a high-paid career with an employer. If you're good enough to command a high salary for the work that you do for your employer, then you're good enough to set up as a consultant and run your own business. If you excel at what you do, it can be more logical to work as a freelancer and enjoy the flexibility and freedom that comes with that.

Franchising is similar to freelancing in that you're in charge of your hours and can grow something that belongs to you. Many successful franchisees have told me that the return on their investment was much more than they anticipated. It's not just about the money, though. They all tell me how much their quality of life has improved as a result of buying into a franchise.

CASE STUDY – LINDA STONE

Linda Stone is a great example of someone who's made a brilliant success of franchising. Linda sacrificed a well-paying career in media because she wanted flexibility and a better quality of life, and she achieved enormous success with the first franchise she invested in.

Linda's franchise was part of the *Families* Magazine. The business model for this franchise relies on delivering advertising sales. It's the sharp end of selling and tenacity, and persistence is required. Linda wasn't prepared to give up until there was a definite 'no', and sometimes not even then! Sales aside, the success of Linda's franchise came down to her ability to add value for clients and retain them long-term.

Linda was so successful with her initial franchise that she went on to lead the whole franchise group. She attributes the success of *Families* magazine, which has been around for thirty years, to its being meaningful to readers. Despite the amount of information available online, many readers of the magazine report that they can browse the internet forever but *Families* magazine curates the best of what's out there, verifies it and delivers it in an easy-to-absorb format for time-poor parents. Ninety-nine percent of *Families* franchisees are parents themselves, working from home around their children. This is a testament to the locally run franchise model where the franchise owner is one of the cohort being served.

Linda's story shows us that with the right franchise model, the energy to grow it and a willingness to put in the hard work, there's no limit on how successful you can become.

Collaborate, don't compete

Collaboration is a keyword in franchising. In the business world you're always competing, either with someone in your area or against similar businesses in the same sector.

Regarding franchising, you're competing with the outside world, but you've got peers on your side on the inside who've got a vested interest in making you more successful. When we hold master franchise brainstorming sessions with our franchisees at Fantastic Services, I see business owners giving each other unmatched degrees of support – this is something that I've never witnessed in a workplace, or even in the best multinational companies.

Let's say a franchise in one area learns that doing X is leading to success. This information – the research, the know-how and the resources – is shared with all the franchisees so that everyone can benefit from the knowledge and grow their business.

Business owners like to talk about their successes, but they don't usually share all the details regarding how they achieve them. In business, you often don't want other businesses to succeed. Inside franchising it's different. It's collaborative rather than competitive. Of course you want to be the best franchise in your group, but you also want to make sure that your peers are successful because that means a higher national or international budget, which will enable you to grow your business even more. When all the franchisees are successful, everyone reaps the rewards, so a support system is built into the business model from day one.

There's also much more teamwork within a franchise than within business departments. I've seen first-hand that even in successful companies, team members often don't collaborate because they're looking for their next promotion. With a franchise, you're in charge of your own promotion, of your own growth, so you don't need to compete with your peers. When everyone in the franchise is successful, you'll make more money as a franchise, and the energy that you have for collaboration and commitment to your peers becomes much higher.

The Olympics of business

Each sport in the Olympic Games has a different set of rules and different equipment. For example, in tennis, the court is always a certain size and shape, and only one type of ball is used. The athletes also wear a particular type of outfit. And a tennis player plays against other tennis players in the same way each time.

This is like franchising. In franchising, you're surrounded by similar businesses you can easily measure yourself against, in the same way that a professional tennis player can measure themselves against their opponents.

Franchises have a like-for-like brand, a like-for-like demographic and like-for-like equipment, so it's easy to see where you stand in relation to the other franchisees. This is what makes a lot of franchises outperform other businesses.

In other types of business you do things your own way. You can research the market and your competitors, of course, but it's not the same as having direct comparisons to learn from.

There will be risks

Everything carries risk. Setting up a business involves risk, being a freelancer involves risk and being an employee involves risk. Every single investment carries a risk. Even keeping cash in your bank is a risk. It's part of the game.

The number one thing I hear people say about franchising is 'It's harder than I thought it was going to be'. This applies to almost everything, though. Almost everything is harder than you think it's going to be.

Whatever you choose to do, there will be risks involved. There will be hard work and downsides. There are of course risks involved in taking on a franchise, but these risks are reduced because you're working with a proven business model and have the ongoing support of your peers.

And if you do decide to give up the franchise for whatever reason, it's likely that one of your fellow franchisees will want to take it over, and you'll make back your initial investment. This isn't usually the case with other types of businesses. Even profitable service businesses can be hard to sell when they don't have a good process – when the owner leaves, they are almost unsellable.

Summary

Hopefully you're beginning to understand just how successful franchises can be and are starting to think about how you might benefit from running your own.

In the next chapter, we'll look at marketing and how knowing the right things to measure, and how to measure them, is key to success in business.

THREE

Marketing: Measure To Maximise

In the previous chapter, we looked at what a franchise is and explored what makes one successful. In this chapter, we're going to focus on marketing and why measuring success is so important for business growth, no matter what type of business you have.

Peter Drucker said, 'the business enterprise has two – and only two – basic functions: marketing and innovation. Marketing and innovation produce results; all the rest are costs.'[5] However, marketing can be a huge

---

5.   Forbes, 'Peter Drucker on Marketing', *Forbes* (3 July 2006), www .forbes.com/2006/06/30/jack-trout-on-marketing-cx_jt_0703drucker .html?sh=9b18fe2555cb, accessed 24 March 2022

waste. I like to see it as a number of steps you have to take, one-by-one, before you can free up the budgets for the really big push and a path that can lead you to being nationwide with a brand so well-known that you are the top choice. This is called having the mind-share, and when you get to this point you will reach critical mass – whenever people think of a service like gardening, they think of your brand first, meaning you will grow without having to spend money on getting new customers.

Rule 1 of Marketing – Keep your customers!

When your product or service is good, you'll get word-of-mouth recommendations, and these are what ultimately help you grow. The goal of marketing is to reach critical mass, which is the point where every customer refers more than one other person to your business. When this happens, you'll see a snowball effect. But getting there from zero isn't easy.

Anyone can spend £20 million on marketing, but the question is whether they can grow a business. The key to growing your business, whatever business you have, is delivering good products or a great service, not spending all your money on advertising. We started Fantastic Services with about £3,000 in our bank account and grew it to, at the time of writing, £30 million annually. That's a huge increase over twelve years, but we didn't grow the business through advertising – we did it by offering fantastic services and gaining lots of word-of-mouth referrals as a result.

When it comes to marketing your business, regardless of the channel you're using, it's critical to measure and manage to maximise. Any marketing campaign that makes more than the initial investment back is a good one and should be repeated. But you won't know how your marketing investments are doing unless you measure the results and manage the campaigns effectively. If you don't measure and can't manage, you will never be able to maximise.

Of course with a franchise, you know you've got a good product because it's been tried and tested. As well, everybody within the business takes responsibility and is accountable for measuring and managing its core functions. I'll talk more about accountability in the next chapter. When accountability is built into the business, it becomes much easier to measure and manage and therefore maximise growth.

First, let's look at the most important reason for marketing: customers.

Rule number 2: Make it easy for customers to find you

Marketing, far from being a cost, is actually an investment in being found. Marketing is about finding customers – or letting them find you.

What I've learned in my over twenty years in business is that the most effective way to market is to be where your customers are. If a customer is asking for something, you need to be exactly where they're asking for it. If they do a Google search for 'cleaners near me', for example, you should be there in the search results. There are plenty of ways to get there. You might choose to read books that will teach you how to do it, or you can hire a dedicated agency like FranchiseFame.com to do it for you.

Nothing beats being where your customer wants you. If you're not on top on the first page of a Google search, you might as well not exist. There aren't many marketing strategies more effective than ranking number one on the Google listings for your local area for a service business.

Of course, once your customers find you, you need to keep them. Do whatever is necessary to keep your customers loyal to you.

The three types of marketing

There are hundreds of different ways to market your product or service, but fundamentally, they boil down to just three types of marketing: offline, online and advertising, or PR, which is above the line marketing – meaning you're building your brand, not selling transactional marketing. The Google research on ZMOT (zero moment of truth), means you have to build a brand and a company that is trusted, and have a number of touch points.

Offline marketing

Offline marketing is about location and visibility. On my https://fantasticbusiness.com/resources website you can download the latest list of places and what the effect is of each, type of marketing, from flyers to postcards to outdoor media. Research by Google suggests that a buyer needs to be consistently visible across a range of locations to build trust.[6] This means when they finally go to make the purchase, they don't hesitate. Your reputation is crucial for your success here; we have seen that consistent branding and visibility increase awareness and create conversion, from

---

6. Think with Google, 'Study reveals the complexity of modern consumer paths to purchase and how brands can make inroads' (June 20018), www.thinkwithgoogle.com/intl/en-cee/consumer-insights/consumer-journey/study-reveals-complexity-modern-consumer-paths-purchase-and-how-brands-can-make-inroads, accessed 27 April 2022

the offline to the online world. And only by utilising several offline and online locations can we increase the conversion. This means the marketing costs become lower the more your brand is recognised and trusted. This is what you would want to achieve.

Online marketing

There are many types of online marketing, but I'm going to focus on three. The first one is SEO, or organic search. I call it discovery, because it's about being found. The second one is paid adverts. The third type is display advertising. This is where you pay for branding on Instagram, Facebook and Google.

I always go straight to online marketing first because it's easy to track (aka measure) and you can straight away see which campaigns are working and which aren't.

Advertising/PR

Advertising can involve taking out big newspaper adverts or paying for radio adverts or even television, but it also involves branding the business rather than simply advertising a straight-up service. It means making your profile and/or your business's profile visible. This can happen via many different channels. There are too many to list, but examples are TikTok, LinkedIn and the metaverse.

The world is constantly changing, and there are new methods and growth hacks coming all the time. The way to stay on top of them is by following the principle of giving customers value, not for how you advertise or where you put banners up but how you attach them to your business. Build an asset of things they need; we have enormous content sections and create valuable useful content that our customers use. Be of value and be where your customers are looking for you. Step into your customer's shoes for a moment, and ask, 'What would be of value for me?' Then give them that.

Marketing Rules by growth hacking

Rule 1: Keep the customer

Nothing is more expensive than losing the customers you have or disappointing them. Anyone can spend money on advertising, but can you deliver?

Rule 2: Be found where your customers look for you

This should be obvious, but a lot of small companies don't know how, and this area is getting harder and harder. This is why big brands have a higher chance of success.

Rule 3: Step-by-step

Start with the lowest cost of acquisition then move up.

If you can't keep your customers, or grow them, then all your efforts are wasted. Having the most famous brand can mean nothing – I know of brands that failed as they spent so much on marketing, but failed to keep the customers.

Rule 4: Add value

Be of value; be an inspirational light for your clients. They don't care about you; they care about what value you can add. Make your customers raving fans; they are part of your success so make them part of your journey.

Rule 5: Accelerate growth

If your cost per acquisition is less than the lifetime value, and you've got smooth operations – go for it and double down on your efforts, as you are in the sweet growth spot.

Rule 6: Be the brand of choice

The goal is to be in the mindshare, so that every time a client thinks of a service you offer, they think of you first and don't even bother searching for alternatives.

Do you know what to measure?

In a business, it's easy to suffer from analysis paralysis, a result of having too much data to measure. In most businesses, there are only a few things that matter. If you track more than six things, for example, you likely won't make progress, so it's important to know exactly what to measure, and how to measure it.[7]

In the early days at Fantastic Services, we were so obsessed with our conversion rate that we forgot to look at the numbers of bookings and leads. This meant that yes, the conversion rate went up, because we were closely monitoring it, but we were actually making 50% less. We had taken our eye off our sales figures because we were focusing our efforts on improving our conversion rates. We learned a big lesson from this.

Another issue was that we were experiencing 10% delays on all our jobs and couldn't figure out what to do about it. We tried extending the travel times between jobs, but this of course meant that less work would be done each day. Eventually we realised that if we focused only on the first job delay for each day and zoomed in on the reasons why this delay had happened, we could get a better idea of how to resolve the problem.

You see, there's no excuse for a delay on the first job. We worked out that if someone was late for their first job of the day, they would be late for every subsequent job. Once we'd figured out how to reduce the delays in getting to the first job, we went from 15% delays to 2%

---

7.   Doerr, J, *Measure What Matters: How Google, Bono, and the Gates Foundation Rock the World with OKRs* (Portfolio, April 2018)

delays – a huge result that came from knowing exactly which key performance indicators (KPIs) to measure.

It's critical for your KPIs to line up with what matters. Make sure you're measuring the stuff that's important for the bottom line. If you're not looking at the right KPIs, you'll make mistakes, and this is why starting a business from scratch can be difficult. In a start-up, you might not know what to measure at first. You only find out through trial and error.

In a franchise, it's easier to understand what KPIs you need to drill down into at each part of the journey because the franchisor will tell you. You'll also have help measuring and managing the data you collect, which leads to faster progress.

All improvement in business happens because you measure progress and implement processes as a result.

Feedback accelerates growth

For prospective franchisees, measurement in the form of feedback is critical. The franchisor should measure what they do and make the franchisee accountable for providing feedback that could help the business.

At Fantastic Services, we built something called 'BettR' (Fantastic Better Rate) to help us get feedback from our customers. The Better Rate is a feedback scorecard we give customers once a job has been done. The customer fills it in, and we're then able to dig down into the feedback to see exactly what happened in that customer's experience. All of this is in the gofantasic app and our app for our professionals, and it's instant.

Feedback is important because it allows you to see what you're doing well and what you need to improve. When you ask your customers what you did well and list specific adjectives, eg 'friendliness', 'punctuality', 'cleanliness' etc, you'll see immediately what you need to work on.

Collecting feedback instantly and connecting it straight to the person giving it also means that you'll be able to make changes right away, and this will help you to improve your business more than anything else.

I used to work as a chef. In this job, there was no delay when it came to getting feedback. A dish would go out and if the customer didn't like it, it came right back. The worst thing in this industry is that chefs and waiting staff often don't see the facial expressions of customers when they're eating the food. If the staff can't see what's really happening, mediocre restaurants are born. And potential customers will be sure to read the mediocre reviews.

The difference between a mediocre restaurant and a great restaurant is the staff's ability to recognise the feedback they see on their customers' faces and act upon it immediately. As a chef, it's hard to be told to redo the dish, or to replate it, but ultimately, it's the feedback process that makes Michelin-starred chefs get to the level they're at.

It's the same with coaches who work with high-performance athletes. They look at the athletes' numbers and know right away whether they performed well. To progress, grow and improve, we need feedback – and the sooner the better.

We built the Better Rate to improve the quality of our work. When we started in the industry, about 14% of our customers complained. I didn't think this was that bad at the time, as it was about average for our industry. I knew that complaints cost money, though, and that providing bad service would mean spending more on advertising to attract clients to replace the ones we lost. I wanted to keep all our customers.

The Better Rate went straight to the heart of the customers' issues. It gave us specific feedback. We saw the rate of complaints drop once we acted on the feedback and started to fix the issues that came up.

You're only as good as the customers who refer their friends

A key metric that every business should look at is its Net Promoter Score (NPS)[8]. The NPS measures whether your customers are raving fans of your business and whether they'll promote it. To use it, simply ask your customer to mark on a scale of 1 to 10 how likely they are to refer you to their friends. If they mark an 8, a 9 or a 10, they're real fans of what you do. A score between 4 and 8 is neutral and anything below a 4 is poor.

Apple has one of the world's highest NPSs. Their fans become brand ambassadors who tell everybody else to buy Apple products and show them off on social media. This is why Apple can charge a premium for their products.

The really successful businesses are the ones that invest in growing their NPS.

Measure to grow

If you're serious about growing your business, you need to measure the KPIs that are relevant to your success. Here are five practical ways to grow your business.

---

8. Qualtrics, 'What is NPS? Your ultimate guide to Net Promoter Score', www.qualtrics.com/uk/experience-management/customer/net -promoter-score, accessed 27 April 2022

1. Work out what really matters. This is the first step. At Fantastic Services, we concluded that for us, the NPS mattered most because everything else kind of fell apart if this didn't stay above a certain threshold.

Whatever really matters for your business, find it and then measure it, even if this means ignoring some of the other things that you think you should be tracking. You can't measure everything, but you *must* measure the things that are vital to your growth.

2. Systemise and digitise. One of the reasons why we double down on IT at Fantastic Services is because we know that in marketing efforts, everything is measurable – but only if you have the correct IT systems in place to do it. Digitising your business will allow you to more easily measure the necessary things, which means you can more easily work out what you need to do to improve. In the chapter about systems, you can read what serviceos.com does and how it helped us grow.

3. Consider the long-term effect. It's important to ask yourself what the long-term effect of measuring a certain KPI will be. 'What happens if I reach that target?' Asking these types of questions will encourage you to think about what you want your business to look like in the future. It will also help you decide if focusing on a particular KPI is worth the time and effort.

4. Don't measure more than six things. As mentioned earlier in the chapter, to avoid analysis paralysis, don't overdo it. Identify the things that are fundamental to your business growth and focus on measuring those. If you're spending all your time generating and analysing data, you won't be able to take the practical steps necessary to grow your business.

5. Use the five whys. This is crucial to the success of your business. I'll talk more about the concept in the next chapter.

MARKETING FORMULA

When you look at the marketing rules, rule number one was keeping your customers and the goal was critical mass, or mindshare.

The formula is your cost per booking compared to the lifetime value.

A customer acquisition value is the cost of getting a new customer. The cost of keeping a customer should be lower than the cost of getting a new customer, that's why you will grow at accelerated rates. Then, if you add more frequency in purchases, you get more repeat purchases as well as more cross sales; the customer buying more or adding services to your skill. At that point, if your average cost per acquisition is less than the lifetime value of a customer, your company is ready for growth.

Critical mass is the point at which you're growing more for pound spent and as long as you have capacity and can keep the NPS and the repeat purchase, you have reached the ultimate growth formula and should be growing.

When you hit critical mass, your customers are coming to you. You don't need to go to them, and your cost per acquisition will go down. As long as your operations are running smoothly, you will be able to serve more customers. We will discuss this further in Chapter 9.

Summary

The marketing world and landscape change rapidly and are becoming more granulated, but the principles stand firm, no matter what the channel is called.

Keep the customer so you can continue to invest in growth. You can only keep your customer if they can find you where they are looking. Then, when you start the journey towards the goal, you take it step-by-step and choose the best types of marketing first. This is where measuring your steps becomes important; a way to avoid the high costs of advertising, but you can add value by becoming famous within your industry, by growing a following that are your raving fans.

When you have this working, you can accelerate growth and really scale your company. You will then be the brand of choice and the customers come to you. Fantastic Services in London now have more searches and visitors than the average monthly for specific services such as carpet cleaning or oven cleaning, meaning we are on the path to reach critical mass.

Now comes the fun part, as marketing is only one side of the business. The rest is about how to innovate and become cost efficient. To really be able to make an impact on this planet, we still have to increase the brand awareness.

In the next chapter, I'll discuss the importance of accountability and we'll examine the five whys.

FOUR

Accountability And Action

In the last chapter, I explained why marketing and managing your KPIs is key to growing a successful business. In this chapter, we'll look at why accountability is just as important.

Accountability and success

As we defined, a business is solving a problem profitably, and wherever there's a problem or a gap, there's a business opportunity. To be successful, a business not only has to solve a problem – it also has to take responsibility for the way it solves that problem.

Taking responsibility means being accountable. If you're not accountable, and if you don't hold others to account, you will never be successful. If you point one finger out, you need to point three fingers back at yourself. That's accountability. It's about not allowing yourself to make excuses. Often we forget we're accountable. For example, in school, the teachers are usually held accountable for our learning. But in fact, it's up to us to do the work.

High-performing athletes know that to win, they've got to put in the hours. They have to hold themselves accountable. Successful people realise that they're ultimately responsible for their performance and don't blame others when things go wrong. This is one of the main differences between those who are successful and those who aren't. A good portion of luck also helps, but it's not something you can plan.

Personal accountability

In any business, you have to set targets and decide how you're going to hit them – and hold yourself accountable for doing so. If something isn't progressing, you need to ask why.

When you hold yourself accountable, you won't just meet your goals – you'll likely achieve them sooner than planned because you've committed to carrying out the necessary actions and know that there are consequences for not doing so.

I've seen it over and over in start-ups, and even in big corporates – the founders, CEOs and senior executives forget that they're ultimately accountable for what they do and what the business does. Numerous issues could be avoided if people at the top of the business realised this sooner.

RECRUIT HELP

Ask family members or friends to hold you accountable – make them part of reaching your goals.

CASE STUDY – DENISE HUTTON-GOSNEY

Denise Hutton-Gosney is the founder of Razzamatazz Theatre Schools and is well known for gaining investment on *Dragons' Den*.

For Denise, accountability runs through every stage of the life cycle of a franchise.

If at one stage the franchisee isn't performing as agreed, the issue needs to be investigated.

Denise is caring and understands that when performance is poor, there's often a mitigating factor, but she explains that you can't let it become an excuse, or a permanent exception. Some of Denise's franchises are geographically close to each other, so if issues with one are allowed to continue, they can quickly escalate and affect the whole region.

If there's no accountability, there are no repercussions for poor performance and one bad apple can soon affect the rest. You might need to have an uncomfortable talk with someone to work out a solution. If a franchisee isn't able to run the business properly, it's much better for them to be open and honest about this. Honesty makes it easier for both franchisor and franchisee to act with the same direction in mind. They're more likely to find a buyer faster and get a good resale value.

Accountability goes both ways.

It's easy to blame others for things that go wrong, to avoid acknowledging that you had a part to play in the problem. You could say that it was a bad season, or that it was difficult to get recruits because nobody wanted to work, but when you make excuses for why something wasn't done or why something failed, guess what happens? Your business doesn't grow, productivity falls and you have lower morale.

If you expect your business to grow without taking accountability for its growth, you're just betting on luck, and luck can be good and bad. It's much better to stake your success on personal accountability.

In the previous chapter, we looked at the importance of measuring certain KPIs. If you make more than one person accountable for a KPI, you end up with a situation where no one is responsible for it – if two people are responsible for something, then no one's responsible.

You need to make sure that accountability for each KPI belongs to only one person and that everyone knows it. It's far too easy to hide behind other people when you don't have sole responsibility for something.

The accountability mirror

David Goggins is a master of physical and mental resilience. In his book *Can't Hurt Me*, he explains that most of us only tap into 40% of our capabilities and sets out a path that anyone can follow to reach their full potential.

One of the ways he turned his life around was with a method he calls 'looking in the accountability mirror'. In his younger years, David was overweight and decided to start running to turn things around. He ended up running ultramarathons and smashing all his running targets because he had an accountability mirror.

Every morning, he'd decide what he needed to do and then look in his bathroom mirror and see that there was no one else there who could achieve it for him. The mirror became a powerful accountability tool for him.[9]

In any business, it's vital to work out what the priorities are. Once you've done that, put them on sticky notes

---

9. Goggins, D, *Can't Hurt Me: Master your mind and defy the odds* (Lioncrest Publishing, 2018)

on your mirror, and every single time you look in that mirror, figure out how you're going to do what needs to be done and recognise that you're the only one who can get you there. This way, you build accountability into your day and become proactive rather than reactive.

Try the accountability mirror method for yourself. Start with three things that you want to achieve in your business and tell yourself that you're going to be accountable for achieving them. Then write them on your mirror. It's a powerful exercise and I promise that doing it will help you to grow your business.

Accountability and franchising

As mentioned, one of the great things about franchises is that accountability is built in. You're accountable to your investors, you're accountable to the franchisor and you're accountable to the other franchisees.

In a franchise, if one area gets a bad review, it reflects on the whole network. A franchise is only as strong as its weakest links, which is why everybody is accountable for raising the standard and the quality of the franchise business.

CASE STUDY – ACTIONCOACH

Brad Sugars founded ActionCOACH in 1993 and almost three decades later it's still the biggest business-coaching franchise worldwide.

ActionCOACH has got to where it is because Brad followed the same principles that I'm setting out in this book. He mastered marketing, was accountable to the business and realised that sales was the biggest game he could play.

He spent a lot of time training both his staff and himself, and accountability was built into the franchise model right from the start. ActionCOACH relies on peer-to-peer accountability, where franchisees compare themselves to others in the franchise. They keep each other on their toes, and it's this accountability that keeps ActionCOACH constantly growing. Once ActionCOACH launched an internal competition, Gary saw that franchises began to perform with even more drive, motivation and focus.

When writing the book, I interviewed Gary Keeting and Kevin Riley, the two best-performing franchisees at ActionCOACH, and for them, it was accountability and their incredible sales processes that were key to their superb results.

In franchising, you're sharing your journey with your peers. Some of them are further along the road than you, some of them are at the same stage and some of them are behind you, but you're all working toward the same goals. There's always going to be someone who's done what you're trying to do, which means you won't repeat problems but will learn from mistakes.

What so many franchisees overlook is the fact that they need to be accountable to themselves. Too often, I've seen franchisees who aren't adequately in touch with the key data sets that underpin their business, most significantly the numbers. I would expect a franchisee to know the call rate, conversion rate, job numbers, income and profit for the preceding day, week and month, and to be alert to how this relates to their business targets.

Most franchisees also have targets that they're expected to reach within a certain time frame. For example, to have their licence renewed, a franchisee will need to have produced a certain amount of growth in the previous year.

This type of accountability isn't in place because the franchise owner wants to take the business away from the franchisee but because they want to help them to grow the business. It keeps them in the habit of working to a standard. You just don't get this type of accountability with a start-up or a corporation. The bonus of course is that with a franchise, you're not just held to account – you're also supported all the way.

It's easy to get distracted in a start-up, perhaps by a new type of marketing or a new way to do things. With a franchise, the distractions are still there but you can't stray too far from your course because you're being held accountable for the growth of the business. You have time frames and targets that will keep you on track and peers to support you in getting there.

More on the importance of feedback

In the last chapter, I talked about why feedback is so important. Feedback is also relevant to accountability. Think of the feedback you receive as your customer's way of holding you to account.

One of the things we discussed in the early days of Fantastic Services was creating a centralised system for feedback in which we could compare like-for-like. Today, one of the reasons why we're growing so fast is that we have an in-built feedback loop, which allows us to stay accountable to our customers. We take feedback on every completed job and immediately give it to our professionals. This allows us to adjust processes and spot trends, as well as improve training if it's single performance issues or systemic across a whole service line.

We can measure feedback instantly, and this means we can target the areas we need to and train the right people at the right time and in the right things rather than just offer the same blanket training to everyone.

It's so important for a franchisee to have constant access to feedback. A franchisor needs to make sure that they devise ways of gathering feedback and to make sure that franchisees can access it.

Most franchises don't have a feedback loop built into them, but I hope that more will in the future. The one we have at Fantastic Services makes us stand out because it's not just about accountability – it's also about having a centralised mission, which will be looked at in greater depth in Chapter 7.

Checklists

Anton Skarlatov, my business partner and CEO of Fantastic Services, is always keen to emphasise how important checklists are for obtaining feedback. A checklist is a way of getting feedback on what you've done and what you've missed in your work.

When you have a business, feedback usually comes in the form of complaints or reviews. In our experience, only about one in ten clients will go to the trouble of complaining. The rest will just go quiet and you'll never know what's wrong. Also, if you receive a complaint, you might not act on it and improve things – if a client is upset, you'll be upset, and it will be difficult to think clearly about a solution.

What we've found is that the best way to get meaningful feedback is to have the client involved in the whole process, and we do this by introducing a checklist. The checklist demonstrates to the client that checks are taking place. It itemises the services that need to be completed. The client can see straight away whether the services were completed and to what standard. This feedback then enables you to improve the service.

A checklist can be simple. For example, if you're a client having a meal, your checklist might ask 'Was your food warm enough?' 'Was there a cherry on top of the cake?' You simply check off the questions that you'd reply with a yes to. Even if the food was average, you'll feel more satisfied having given feedback.

CASE STUDY – SWIMTIME

A good example of a franchise with built-in feedback is Swimtime. The franchise increased its performance and its service by incorporating feedback into the business, by having checklists after the swimming lesson, as well as during the franchise reviews. Swimtime uses technology as a tool to help it outperform, but it's by having clarity over the feedback and performance of each franchise that CEO Theo Millward can see immediately where in the business the franchisees have blind spots and can do what's needed to improve things. This led to the franchise's satisfaction score doubling.

Radical candor

In his book *Cross-Cultural Business Behavior*, Richard Gesteland talks about direct and indirect cultures and how people from indirect cultures find it more difficult to give honest feedback because offering even constructive criticism can be viewed as rude.[10]

If people are insincere in their feedback, though, it's not useful or meaningful. In *Radical Candor*, Kim Scott explains that we can create better relationships in the workplace by encouraging a culture where employee feedback is asked for and valued.

The best way to give feedback is with what Scott calls 'radical candor'.[11] Radical candor is about giving honest feedback sensitively and in a way that allows the other party to change. Scott writes, 'Imagine you see a colleague with their fly undone. In this situation, radical candor might involve taking them aside and telling them quietly that their fly is down. You help them to make the necessary change without making them feel bad or drawing attention to the issue.'

The best leaders are those who encourage their teams and their customers to give feedback with radical candor. Every business needs to hear honest feedback to grow.

10. Gesteland, R, *Cross-Cultural Business Behavior: A guide for global management* (Samfundslitterature Press, 2012)
11. Scott, K, *Radical Candor: How to get what you want by saying what you mean* (Pan; Main Market edition, 2019)

The five whys

When it comes to accountability, the five whys are critical. Earlier, I mentioned that if you point one finger out, you need to point three back at yourself. You can make sure this happens through the five whys.

Let's say you run a large department and have someone doing recruitment, someone doing marketing, etc. It can be easy to blame those individuals every time something goes wrong in their area. Often, though, they aren't the ones accountable. The five whys will help you to uncover the real issues, so you can fix them.

The concept was developed by Sakichi Toyoda.[12] Put simply, any business problem can be understood by asking no more than five questions. For example, if you weren't making enough sales, you'd begin by asking, 'Why aren't I making sales?' You determine that your marketing isn't good enough. So you go deeper and ask, 'Why isn't my marketing good enough?' The marketing manager wasn't trained properly. So you ask, 'Why wasn't my marketing manager trained properly?' and so on.

You never need to ask 'Why?' more than five times, and the questions will ultimately point to you. Either something you're doing or something you haven't

---

12. Mind Tools Content Team, '5 Whys: Getting to the root of a problem quickly', Mind Tools, www.mindtools.com/pages/article/newTMC_5W.htm, accessed 24 March 2022

done is causing the issue. Once you see that you're the one who's accountable, you can fix things. It's a great method for quickly drilling down into the heart of the issue.

Here's another example.

Issue: My business didn't grow this year.

1. *Why didn't it grow?* Because I didn't have enough staff.

2. *Why didn't I have enough staff?* Because I didn't put the ads up on time.

3. *Why didn't I put the ads up on time?* Because I didn't expect the season to start so early.

4. *Why didn't I expect the season to start so early?* Because I didn't read the ops manual.

5. *Why didn't I read the ops manual?* Because I thought I was going to be informed and managed, and not take the responsibility myself.

Now try it for yourself. Think about the last thing that went wrong in your business. Ask yourself why it went wrong. You'll probably find that the first answer you come up with is an excuse, but if you dig deeper and keep asking why, you'll get to the root of the issue. You may not need to ask the question five times to get the fingers pointing at you.

You'll always end up uncovering something that you should change. This exercise is about you as a leader, a manager, a business owner, a franchisee, a franchisor. It's about opening yourself up, looking at what you're doing wrong and then making the changes you need to.

Summary

Without accountability, you will never grow your business or grow as an individual. Use the techniques discussed in this chapter to identify the things you need to fix – and then fix them. Again, if you blame others, you don't grow.

In the next chapter, we'll look at sales and simplicity, which are key to growing a business that's relevant, profitable and progressive.

FIVE
Sales And Simplicity

In the previous chapter, we explored why accountability is so important in business and looked at the concept of the five whys. In this chapter, I'm going to talk about the importance of simplicity in the sales process.

Fantastic customer service

In the past, many people preferred shopping in a store to browsing online because in a store, there are agents who can guide you through the sale. It's obvious that a shop which provides good service to its customers will be more successful than one that doesn't, so staff are carefully trained to ensure consistency and good customer service across all the shop's outlets.

Now, many face-to-face interactions have been replaced by websites, but that doesn't mean that customer service has become any less important. In fact, the most successful businesses are the ones who've managed to replicate good face-to-face interactions on the web.

When a customer is browsing in a shop, they can ask the shop assistant questions about the product or service and have a conversation about whatever it is they're buying. The only way to do this online is to make everything simpler. Online businesses need to simplify their customers' experience of shopping with them by making the interaction into a process where customers feel they're getting a service, not just making a booking. This was the focus of Fantastic Services when we started out in the 2010s.

Taking the perspective of a customer, I ran a test to see how easy it was to find a carpet cleaner in my area. In an online search, I found ten carpet cleaners but none of them displayed their price or availability, and I couldn't see if they offered extra services and how much those might cost. I had to make phone calls to find the answers to my questions.

None of the first three I called answered. I called a few more and eventually got hold of one of them. They told me they couldn't give me a quote over the phone. So I arranged a time for them to come to my place and on the day, they never showed up. I called them again and they came out the next day and quoted me an excruciatingly high price, and that's when I thought, 'There's got to be a simpler way to do this for both the client and for the company'. That thought is what inspired Fantastic Services.

As we looked at how we could improve things for customers, we realised we had to start from scratch. We had to reinvent everything about how a cleaning company worked because we knew that customers wanted to see availability, timing and pricing. As a consumer, I wanted to be able to press a button and book a service at a time and price that I was happy with.

Now, more than 60% of our customers are booking the services they need online, which is incredible given that it's traditionally been a phone-driven business. We could reach 100%, but we have services that we haven't yet seen the benefit of taking online only bookings. The great thing about this for us is that we have more direct bookings than our competitors simply because we've simplified the process. Our way is simpler and quicker, and we're growing fast as a result.

**FIVE STEPS TO BECOMING A
SUCCESSFUL SERVICE COMPANY**

1. Answer the request
2. Give accurate pricing upfront
3. Manage expectations
4. Turn up to the appointment
5. Offer the customer five-star service so they'll come back again.

Simple simply sells.

Successful businesses simplify the process

A sale isn't just about the delivery of the service – it's about the whole end-to-end process. Companies that deliver end-to-end service well include Amazon and Apple. Both make it easy for people to rebuy from them. Companies that reduce the number of barriers between the customer and the purchase do better than ones whose buying process is longer, more complicated or more frustrating.

In *The Big Red Fez*, Seth Godin explains that customers don't want to waste time going in circles trying to find what they want,[13] so remember, your customers aren't there to investigate your service. They don't care about

---

13. Godin, S, *The Big Red Fez: Zooming, evolution, and the future of your company* (Free Press, 2002)

who you are. They're there to make a purchase and you need to make this as easy as possible for them.

One of the best books on this topic is *Don't Make Me Think*, by Steve Krug.[14] I met Steve many years ago at a small seminar on user experience, where he spoke about how the more barriers you can eliminate in a business, the more likely you are to make the sale. Steve, and many others in User Experience Design, inspired me to follow a journey in making Fantastic Services the simplest booking there is; we had the goal to make a process that could book anything anywhere and show realtime availability and price.

CASE STUDY - CLAYTON TRELOAR - SALES

I interviewed Clayton Treloar, CFE of Mail Boxes Etc (Australia) and a Certified Franchise Executive. He bought the Perth franchise, and when he took over he soon realised that the thing that mattered the most was sales. With this recognition he applied a simple methodology; he looked at where his clients were and identified how he could provide value to them.

Clayton knew that he'd be most likely to get sales from the local business community but that going in and delivering sales pitches was only going to work in the short-term. Instead, he spent time establishing his network and donating his knowledge to help the

---

14. Krug, S, *Don't Make Me Think: A common sense approach to web usability* (New Riders; 2nd edition, 2005)

businesses in this network solve problems they had with other non-printing times and to network with other local businesses, and he got a better service by helping with graphic design issues. Because he'd spent time with his customers, he knew what their problems were and was able to assist them. This is what sales is, and it's this approach that made Clayton so successful. Within three months he'd tripled the sales of his store.

A successful franchisee is someone who's either a great salesperson or someone who hires one in. There's no way around this.

Operations manuals keep things simple

Linda from *Families* magazine, whom we met in Chapter 2, said that one of the things that surprised her about the franchise industry is the fact that there's an operations manual. Most companies don't have these, but for a franchise business, they're absolutely essential. Simplicity is embedded within a franchise business because the processes are already simplified and well-rehearsed and have been presented to the franchisee in the operations manual. You have to be able to deliver the same service over and over, and the operations manual explains how to do this.

It's not just franchises that use operations manuals, though. The really successful businesses, such as Starbucks and Apple, for example, have operations manuals that lay out exactly how their stores need to operate. A new Apple store isn't opened randomly – the process is well-planned and highly detailed, and the ways in which the store must be stocked, the staff trained and the products displayed are all set out within the operations manual.

Get creative

The simplest things tend to be the most engineered things. When you look at an iPhone, it's a black slate that seamlessly connects case with the screen and when you open it, the design guides you through the installation and start-up process. When I got my first computer, a Commodore 64, you turned it on and it was ready...you had to instruct it what to do next. Now the simplicity and ease of transferring data from one phone to another on an iPhone and, in my case, the simplicity of booking a carpet cleaning in your area, are results of hours, even years of experience, research and hard work. Think about it, only a few years ago, with the revolution of the iPod, you could have 1,000 songs in your pocket! Now you can open an app and within an hour or two you can have your carpet cleaned and have paid online. This simplicity is a process of a decade of design.

So, to simplify a product or a service, you have to be creative. This means being able to flip the problem upside down. You have to dive into it from several angles to discover what you can do differently to solve it. You need to ask, 'How can I make my process for doing this better than everybody else's?' Consider figuring out who's already done it well and building on that. You could look at how to reduce the number of clicks in the process, for example.

There are still so many possibilities around being creative online. After all, the internet has been around for only twenty years or so. Many app interfaces are still pretty crude, and we'll see things become simpler as the technology develops.

What I want to achieve with Fantastic Services is a process whereby you can say to Alexa or Siri, 'I'm moving out the 22nd', and our app would automatically schedule the packers, the cleaners, the transferral of utility bills. etc. At present you can, 'Ask Gofantastic to book a cleaner at 4pm on Friday'. We've built this capability into our business but are still in the early days of user interface. Like Fantastic Services, the best businesses are those which have an ongoing creative approach to problems. They're the ones continually improving their customers' experiences.

Every single company that simplifies will be more successful.

CASE STUDY – AMAZON AND AIRBNB

Amazon is a good example of a company that's made it its mission to simplify the customer experience. Amazon wants you to buy multiple things when you shop, so just like a bricks-and-mortar shop, the website is divided into sections and it recommends complementary products that you may be interested in. Tabs along the top of the webpage guide you through the store. Amazon has simplified and streamlined its processes because it knows that this is the best way to retain customers and encourage them to buy.

Airbnb has revolutionised the hotel industry by making the process of exploring places to stay, booking one and picking up the key as straightforward as possible, even for people who have low budgets. It makes complicated things simple. Unsurprisingly, the founder of Airbnb comes from a design and UX background.

With Airbnb, it's not just about the bookings. It's also about the quality of the service hosts provide to their guests. Just like any other network, Airbnb is only as successful as its hosts, and it has created a simple way for hosts and guests to communicate.

There is a lot we can learn from these companies.

Simplifying franchises

If you're a franchisee and your franchisor hasn't simplified things for you, do it yourself, as long as it doesn't compromise any legal obligations. The same goes for any business, but with a franchise, if you can help to simplify the process, the whole franchise benefits, so you'll be supported in your work.

It goes back to the two-way support, whereby the franchisor supports the franchisee by having the research and understanding the network and the franchisee supports the franchisor by making sure they offer relevant, constructive feedback on how to improve the business, including how to make things simpler. Every single thing that's done in a franchise has to be done over 1,000 times or more, so even a small simplification can make a huge difference to the business. If you keep things simple, you'll scale faster.

Every complication creates a frustration point. Simply put, the cost of not simplifying is frustration. One little frustration might be viewed as just a bump, but with the second and third frustrations, the bump becomes a hill and then a mountain – in other words, a breaking point.

TOP TIPS FOR SIMPLIFYING YOUR BUSINESS

1. **Invest in training**. The more you train your team, and the more prepared you are in the way that you train, the more you'll level out those bumps in the road. When you employ new people, induct them into the company properly because an hour's training early on will save you ten hours of trying to sort out issues later.

2. **Use systems to simplify**. Never introduce new systems for the sake of it – only for the sake of creating simplicity. If the new system doesn't make things simpler, don't run with it. Also, when you introduce new systems, make sure they're manually tested before they're introduced to customers.

3. **Focus on sales.** Everything you do in your business should be aimed at generating new leads and more sales. At the end of the day, what matters are the sales and the bookings. Don't forget this.

4. **Cut the clicks.** The shorter the route to purchasing, the more efficient your business. Every single click can create frustration. The more clicks you eliminate, the smoother and simpler the process will be and the more customers you'll keep.

5. **Evaluate the speed of your processes.** Certain things in your processes might be slow and add no value – the verification of documents, for example. You need to cut down on these types of processes to speed things up. Conversely, training can be slow, but it adds value, so it needs to stay.

6. **Act like a customer.** As both Steve Krug and Seth Godin advise, step inside the shoes of your customer and look at things from their perspective. I also suggest being grumpy when you do this! Approach everything as if you're a customer having a bad day. What things are going to make your day worse? What can the business do to make your day better?

Find the right people for sales

Some people are more natural salespeople than others, and although most can be trained to become good at sales, not everyone wants to be. You need to find the salespeople who can help your business and invest in them because at the end of the day, a business is sales.

My business partner Anton believes that if you don't feel comfortable selling, you should hire someone to perform that business function. This isn't just the case for sales but for every area within the business. If you're not good at managing people, hire someone who is good at that.

The worst thing you can do is spend time learning how to do something you're not skilled at and don't want to do. Your time would be better spent hiring someone else to do it and focusing on the things that you are good at and are interested in.

Summary

Simplicity is necessary to grow a successful business. Always put yourself in your customers' shoes and think through each step of the purchasing process. What can you cut out to make things smoother? Can you reduce the barriers? If you do this, your clients will keep coming back.

In the next chapter, I'm going to talk about teams and training them.

SIX

Training And Talent

In the last chapter, I talked about simplicity and its role in sales. In this chapter, I'm going to discuss the role of your team in your business.

The importance of training

Richard Branson says, 'Train people well enough so they can leave, treat them well enough so they don't want to.'[15]

The reason we in Fantastic Services invest in training is the answer to this question.

---

15. Branson, R, (@richardbranson) 'Train people well enough...' (27 March 2014), https://twitter.com/richardbranson/status /449220072176107520?lang=en, accessed 27 April 2022

'What happens if you train your staff, and they leave?'

'What happens if you don't train them, and they stay?'

A business's success depends on people, and their performance depends on experience and training, and training is a fundamental obligation of a franchisor. Franchisors need to support the franchisee to succeed and make sure they represent the brand as required. They do this by transferring knowledge of processes and procedures. It's also a fundamental responsibility of a franchisee to do the same with their staff.

Your company is only ever as good as the people you're working with. It's always better to spend time and money training your staff than not to. It's really very simple: if you don't train your staff, your business will fail.

What you're looking for is synergy – which will drive business growth – and that comes from having the right recruitment practices in place and getting the right people in, but it also comes from providing your people with the right training.

Success in any business involves understanding whether people are performing and what can be done to help them to perform better, and then continuously providing them with opportunities to improve.

Getting to know your team

In *Radical Candor,* Kim Scott uses the terms 'rock star' and 'superstar' to describe two types of people in business.

The difference between them is clear. The superstar wants to jump from department to department, work in different roles and functions and reach a higher level in their career. The rock star, on the other hand, is very, very good at their job, and if you move them out of it, you're going to lose core strengths. To have a successful business, you need to identify what type of people you employ, where they are in their career with you and where their ambitions lie. You need to find your superstars and rock stars and support them to work in the way that best suits them because only then will they bring true value to your business.[16]

You always have to know your people. You have to know what their desires are and what their personal investment in your company is. Know why they're investing their time with you. What do they want to achieve?

The magic happens when you couple the personal goals of your team members with your business goals. When these goals merge, you'll have a team that will achieve much more than they thought possible.

---

16. Scott, K, *Radical Candor* (Pan, 2019)

TOP TIPS FOR GETTING TO KNOW YOUR TEAM

1. **Have regular personal conversations**. Be on time and respect the person. It's not a telling-off session but a chance to find out about the people on your team. I often like to do this during a walk, as being outside of the work setting will encourage your team member to open up more.

2. **Listen more than you talk**. Think of the acronym WAIT: 'Why am I talking?' If you're talking more than you're listening, stop and shift your focus back to your team member.

3. **It's about them**. This is not a results-update meeting, or an appraisal or a disciplinary – this is about understanding your team member. It's about them as a person and their goals. It's really important that the one-to-one doesn't turn into a numbers update.

4. **Take notes**. Make sure you understand their situation and whether there are things that the person needs your help with, or something that they need in order to meet their personal goals. Write things down so that you don't forget. You need to be proactive, and you can't take action if you've forgotten what you need to do.

5. **Take action**. Hold yourself accountable to your team members and make sure you do what you can to support them in their careers and personal goals.

The one-to-one

When you meet with your team members for their one-to-ones, you want them to feel comfortable enough to open up to you about what's going on in their life in general. This will help you understand more about their work performance and how you can support them. If someone is having a difficult time at home, for example, they might not be performing well at work.

The best way to make them feel comfortable is to ask open, non-threatening questions and to make sure that not all of the questions are work related.

Don't judge, criticise or tell them what to do. Remember that you're there to listen.

QUESTIONS TO ASK IN THE ONE-TO-ONE
- What's on your mind?
- How happy were you this past week?
- Did anything upset you this week?
- How productive were you?
- What feedback do you have for me as a manager?

How many people are you managing?

In my experience, you can only directly manage nine people effectively at any one time. The ideal number is seven – realistically, it's the largest number of people you can have a meaningful one-to-one relationship with. Seven people means seven hours a week as a minimum, that's about how much quality you can get with your reports.

Once you get to the point where you're managing more than nine people, you either have to employ another manager, promote someone or become extremely effective with your one-to-ones.

When people perform badly, it's often because their focus is elsewhere. It's your job as their manager to help them shift that focus back to where it should be or help them to move into an area that might suit them better. You can't do this if you're managing lots of people because you won't have time to do the one-to-ones necessary to uncover the problem.

Measuring team performance

In Chapter 3, I talked about the importance of measuring performance against KPIs. When it comes to a team member, poor performance usually comes down to one or more of these things:

1. They haven't been trained well enough to do their job.

2. They've got personal issues that are getting in the way.

3. They don't have the resources to do their job properly.

4. They don't understand the purpose of their role, or where they fit into the business.

5. They have lost motivation – remember motivation isn't optional. Even your own.

It's important to find out which of these things is the case, and that's where the one-to-ones will help you. If you've investigated and none of them apply, then it's most likely a fifth reason: they're not a good fit for your company and need to be let go.

The first four issues can be resolved, or understood. The last cannot, and you have a duty to your company, to your team and to the individual to not carry them if they'd be better off working somewhere else.

Meaningful training

Training happens when your team members trade their time for education and experience. If they're not receiving any benefit from the training, it's not real training – it's just a waste of their time and they'll resent it.

You need to offer training, and it needs to be meaningful. More and more training is moving online, and unfortunately it can look like a tick-box exercise. If you watch *MasterChef* or a MasterClass on cooking, you're not going to become a much better cook. If you're already skilled at it you might pick up one or two things, but this type of passive education isn't going to help you leave a legacy. When you train people, as much as possible, move it away from the screen and into the classroom.

There are always discussions on the efficiency of recollection of material taught in an online training course. If the sessions are recorded, nobody can ask questions and you can't tell whether people are focused and engaged. There should always be an element of the training that's live, even if it's not in person. Test and measure the results of all the training you do, to find what works best for you and your team.

Training has to be constant and should be repeated. Effective training happens when you add the personal touch of the one-to-ones, dig deep into results and take time to understand how your team members will overcome the blocks preventing them from working at the level they should be.

To measure the results of your training, use a checklist.

The training checklist

The training checklist will give you the data you need to further develop your training to make sure that it stays relevant and useful to your team.

This is a simple checklist that you can use in your business.

1. Did the training have the outcome you expected? If no, continue and ask the following questions:

2. Was it the student?

3. The teacher?

4. The materials?

5. The delivery method?

6. The examination? Or how you tested results?

7. The timing?

Change what you need and revise. Don't train for the sake of training. Train for outcome and results. Training doesn't have to be a chore. Training should be tied into the outcome, not just for your business, but also for the employee and pro. Ask yourself, what's in it for me? For them? Remember the why. If training is simply about compliance, then that is all you'll get. But if training is about the purpose, you will get more than just the training out of it, so always train for culture.

It's important to ask your team for feedback on the training that you provide, so you can keep developing it. At Fantastic Services, we ask for feedback all the time to improve our training and the results of it.

You're never stronger than your weakest people

Most companies have a number of functions, including marketing, sales, customer service, operations, finance and IT. If one of these teams is failing, your company won't be stronger than that team.

That said, in a franchised business, some of the functions have divided responsibilities. This is where a franchise can be stronger than other types of businesses and the shared growth and documented processes can contribute to the learning and the feedback growth.

When you have an underperforming team, you're either going to have other teams taking over that team's functions, which means that they're no longer performing to their highest capabilities, or the underperforming part of the business will simply continue to fail and bring the rest of the business down with it.

There's no point having the best marketing if you're not making sales to the leads you're getting. There's no point making sales if you're not taking the money in.

Real teamwork involves different functions working together across the business.

In a case where someone is out of the office, you need to be able to leave it to the team to take care of everything in their absence. If they can't, then you haven't trained them well enough. As a leader, you have to make yourself redundant. That's the goal. You do this through training.

CASE STUDY – FANTASTIC SERVICES

At the beginning, retention in our call centre was low. It wasn't a salary issue, it wasn't an issue with the environment and it wasn't an issue with the perks and benefits. It was simply that there was no career path.

When there's no career path, you perform your function but don't move up. The people at the call centre, especially the young ones, quickly got tired of not being able to progress within the business and wanted to move to a new company for the sake of having more challenges.

Once we'd addressed this by creating a career path for our team members, we went from having a churn rate of almost 30% to 70% – one of the lowest churns you can have in a call centre – and we're proud of that.

Why franchises solve talent problems

The franchise is a system, and all its functions, including training, are systemised. This makes recruitment for a franchise easy – it's clear what sort of person is needed to fulfil each function and what type of training they need.

As I've mentioned, with the operations manual, you've already got the training solution in front of you. You need to follow it and make sure that your staff know what the expectations of them are.

The franchise can also solve the talent problem by seconding team members from one franchise business into a different one. The business which needs help gets it, and the person being seconded also has the opportunity to learn from working in a different business.

It bears repeating: the wonderful thing about franchises is that so much trial and error is avoided. This applies to staffing a franchise as well.

Lose the people who aren't a good fit

For many years my father was a talent manager for a large software company. One of the most important things he learned is that once you've decided to let a person go, you can never let them go too soon.

My advice is to give people three chances to improve, but never let them have more then one quarter of the year under performing. After that, let them go, otherwise you'll end up spending more time and energy on managing them than you will on the people who are a good fit.

It's crucial to weed out the people who aren't right for the business because ill feeling spreads quickly. It's almost exponential. One bad person in a team of seven can make the whole team perform much worse. This is because resentment builds. As the boss, you'll lose the respect of your other employees if they see that you're not dealing with issues and don't value the work of the team enough to remove the barriers to its success.

The good thing about franchises is that it tends to be much easier to measure poor performance, which means that you can more quickly spot whether someone is suitable or not.

Measure, feedback, train

Training is about creating habits that produce a better result consistently.

One of the most important things that we did in Fantastic Services was create a 'measure, feedback, train' loop regarding people's performance. As I've said, it's critical to measure performance, and when you're called Fantastic Services, it's even more important to make sure that you're delivering the best service possible. We had a lot to live up to.

Along with measuring performance, you also have to offer your team feedback on the results and train them so that they can help you improve business performance. We use software to gather feedback from clients, but we also check in on the operatives to make sure they're hitting their KPIs. As soon as customer feedback is poor, or an operative fails to meet a specific KPI, we put interventions in place to address this.

The important thing here is the speed of the feedback. You need to gather the evidence and then offer feedback in a constructive way, and quickly, if you want to see business performance improve. You then need to provide training straight away to avoid the same issues happening again.

Think back to the example of the chef. The best way to improve is to get immediate feedback. When there's a long time between offering a service and receiving feedback on that service, it's harder to change things because poor practices have been allowed to continue and may have become ingrained.

Similarly, if you let too much time pass between receiving the feedback and training your team, you'll lose the sense of urgency and things likely won't change.

Another thing to understand is that any training that's delivered isn't really delivered until the new results are in. If the training hasn't brought up the quality of your service, then it hasn't worked. Only the results of the training matter, not the training itself.

Why managers need to be proactive in training

To return to Kim Scott's analogy, when managers recognise the difference between a rock star and a superstar and understand that you can't have more than one bad quarter in a year. By focusing on having no more than one bad quarter as a practice, a sense of urgency and accountability will be created, as we discussed in Chapter 4, and managers will automatically become more proactive about training their teams.

The goal of the training should be to help team members become either rock stars or superstars. The best managers will be watching everyone in their team and will work out where each person is heading before the person even understands it themselves. This understanding can be developed through the one-to-one meeting process I spoke about earlier. When you really know your team, and the individuals within it, you'll be much more able to predict where they're headed and where they should be headed.

Remember, though, that every individual can't run at 100% all the time. It's important to know when to push, when to pull and when to support. Again, this comes back to the importance of having regular one-to-ones with your team members. When you know what's going on in their personal lives and working relationships, you'll know when the time is right to push them and when you need to back off and give them support.

TOP TIPS FOR TRAINING

1. **Have regular one-to-ones with your team members**. Listen and remember it's about them, not you.

2. **Identify their career path and help them understand it and where they are on their journey**. Allow them to change the pathway if they're not happy.

3. **Remember that the training itself isn't what's important but the results of the training**.

4. **Make sure there's a follow-up** – there's no point having people sit through a ten-hour online course if it doesn't have an impact on their needs.

5. **Mix it up**. Take your team members to a different location for the training and/or ensure there's a mix of face-to-face and online (live and recorded) training. Your team will thank you for the variety and will focus more on the content as a result.

Summary

Hopefully this chapter has shown you why it's so important to understand everyone on your team. If you don't know your team members, you won't be able to support them to achieve their full potential, or understand the reasons why they might be underperforming.

You also need to ensure that you're measuring performance, gathering feedback and acting on that feedback to train your team.

In the next chapter, I'll discuss why every business needs a clear purpose.

SEVEN

Essence, Passion and the Why

In the last chapter, I talked about teams and training them. In this chapter, I'll talk about the importance of having a purpose and why your business needs one.

The purpose-driven business

A long-term sustainable business, in terms of sustainability for the planet, but also in the business environment, is one that realises it has a responsibility to others, makes solid foundations in accountability and enrols staff and partners in the mission of the company.

To understand this, work backwards and think about a business which is truly great, a business you admire, and try to work out how it got to be where it is. You'll find that the one thing all the truly great businesses have in common is that they're not passion driven – they're purpose-driven. I would give examples of purpose-driven businesses, but it's your definition of success that matters. Look at two companies in the clothing industry for example. Gymshark, a fast fashion disposable clothing consumer brand, and Patagonia, who focus on sustainable clothing for the great outdoors – protecting what they have at heart by making clothes that retain and protect the earth. The first grew very fast, based on incredible marketing skills and the other took a long time. They have roughly the same market value, however it's your definition of where you would like to lead and what drives you. Who you work for, and with, your choices as a consumer, as a leader, and what you decide your responsibility to the planet is, that completes your definition of success. Our definition at Fantastic Services is simple: we don't have unlimited time on the planet and our kids and grandchildren should have the chance to see nature thrive alongside us. This might be a longer journey, and it may be harder, but we no longer have the choice, it's our responsibility to leave this planet in a better state.

Purpose-driven businesses understand that they have a responsibility to others. When your purpose is to make things better, and you believe in that purpose, you'll put in the hard work to grow your business. Your purpose will give you the stamina and the drive to push through when things seem to be working against you.

Another great thing about having a purpose is that it helps everyone on the team understand the 'why' of the business. When everybody understands why you're doing what you're doing, they'll get behind it and all pull in the same direction.

At Fantastic Services, we work with the principle of 360 degrees of happiness. This is our way of describing the relationship our business has with our stakeholders and reminds us to think about our owners, employees, partners, people and the planet in everything that we do.

The 360 degrees of happiness resulted from our asking ourselves, 'Why are we doing what we're doing?' We first concluded that we did it for the stakeholders, then came to the understanding that it's not just owners who are stakeholders. Everyone involved, and even the planet itself, is a stakeholder.

When we do business, we need to always think of the planet as a stakeholder. We've done numerous things to make the business more sustainable and have less environmental impact. When we design new features, or develop new services or processes, we always take the planet into account. This is why we call it 360 degrees of happiness – it's a full circle, a 360-degree marketplace, not just a win for the customers. We cannot design one-sided services that benefit only one type of stakeholder.

We understand that a franchise is driven by the people in the franchise network. A sustainable franchise understands the value of these stakeholders and makes sure that they're considered.

Principles vs purpose

We decided early on in Fantastic Services that we wanted to be strict about the types of business we worked with, and for us, that meant not working with any businesses related to addiction (gambling businesses or ones which sell alcohol, for example).

Our purpose is an environmental one. We provide cleaning, repairing and maintenance services – a clean carpet will always be better than a carpet that goes to landfill. Fantastic Services was founded on having a responsibility to the environment, and that's what makes us a sustainable business.

Fast fashion is everywhere. As a society, we're replacing our stuff faster and faster. Clothes, furniture, electronics – pretty much everything we buy gets replaced quickly, and we see this as a huge problem. We wanted to do our bit to combat the wastefulness that we see in the world, so we aligned ourselves with sustainable services. Our purpose is about making the planet a better place, and that's where cleaning, maintenance and repair come in. Doing these things means a reduction in waste.

Because everybody within our company understands and pursues the same purpose, we're able to grow and expand into other sustainable areas, such as rainwater collection, cavity insulation, non-cavity wall insulation, solar-power installation and LED replacements, for example. We've also added appliance repairs and hard-surface repairs to our services. The shared purpose gives us our drive, and it's something that our customers can understand and appreciate.

Another thing that makes Fantastic Services stand out from other franchises is the fact that we think about the miles our franchisees travel. Most franchises don't consider this, or understand why it matters. We know that cutting driving time means less idle time and therefore more sales, but it also means fewer CO_2 emissions. So reducing the number of miles travelled aligns with our purpose.

Traditionally, franchises operate within large geographical areas, and the franchisees might not always live close to their business. What we do differently at Fantastic Services is take the home postcode of the franchisee as our starting point and build out their operating area from that. By taking this approach, we've managed to reduce the number of miles driven by our franchisees by 38%. This has been great for us, as it's enabled us to take on more jobs, but more importantly it's helped the environment too. You can see why purpose is so important to successful businesses. Purpose drives innovation and innovation drives growth.

Franchising and the community

A common misconception about franchising is that a franchise is a big global company that owns something that it sells. This isn't true. Franchises are locally run businesses that employ local people. Yes, the franchise headquarters receives a royalty fee, but everything else stays in the community. The way that we've reduced the miles our franchisees have to drive ties in with this, as all our franchisees live and work within the same community.

Businesses which are local tend to be better at community engagement because they have a better understanding of their community business network. They're better placed to do charity work, for example, because they understand local needs and how to contribute in a meaningful way. This is different from a centrally driven company far removed from the community within which it's located. The franchise brand might be national, or even global, but the individual franchise is always a local business, and this is important to remember.

CASE STUDY – DIDDI DANCE

diddi dance is a locally run business, and Anne-Marie Martin, the founder, is passionate about dance. She spent a good twelve years figuring out how she could build her career within dance. Now, what she's doing with her franchise is taking that learning and passing it on so that she can help others run local dance businesses.

Anne-Marie has a clear purpose that's bigger than her business. She knows that many children aren't active enough and that one of the best ways to get them active, and also laughing and enjoying themselves, is through dance.

This isn't about having a seven-figure business. It's about providing people who have a passion for something with an opportunity to build a business based around that passion. The children, their parents and the community all benefit from having the diddi dance business in their local area, but the franchisee benefits most of all because they're earning money doing something they love while also pursuing a higher purpose.

Passion vs purpose

In *Can't Hurt Me*, David Goggins talks about passion-driven motivation.[17] One of the things he says is that passion is fleeting, whereas purpose lasts forever. Motivation is easy to lose if you hit a hurdle. If the temperature is cold, for example, your motivation to run outside diminishes. Again, purpose is much bigger.

---

17. Goggins, D, *Can't Hurt Me: Master your mind and defy the odds* (Lioncrest, 2020)

Passion is dopamine driven. It's fickle. Purpose is much more of a driver and isn't easily lost.[18]

A group of people who share the same passion can be a powerful thing, but your company will become much stronger if the people who work for you share your purpose because they understand it, they believe in it and don't see themselves as working for you but for the purpose.

Tesla is a good example of a business founded on a clear purpose. Elon Musk is happy about competition and wishes more car manufacturers would start producing electric cars. He's said that he doesn't even care if they outsell him because if they do, then he's succeeded in his 'ideological motivation', which is to stop human extinction.[19]

Passion allows you to become a key person of influence, and for your business to become a key company of influence. When you transform from passion to purpose and harness the power of having a clear purpose and people pulling together in the same direction, you can have a much bigger impact on the planet.

18. Goggins, D, *Can't Hurt Me: Master your mind and defy the odds* (Lioncrest Publishing, 2020), https://davidgoggins.com/book, accessed 27 April 2022

19. Lachance Shandrow, K, 'Elon Musk tells Tesla competitors to bring it on', *Entrepreneur* (28 September 2015), www.entrepreneur.com /article/251129, accessed 27 April 2022

We all want to give something back. We all want to help our communities. When we do that as a collective, with a shared purpose, we're much stronger.

Move forward with your 'why' in mind

We asked numerous commercially driven franchise companies to share their 'why' with us, and they all said it was freedom. Similarly, freedom is one of the big drivers for people leaving the corporate world. They want to go out there and do things for themselves.

I always say that this is step one of the journey, finding your 'why'. Someone might want to be in business for themselves for freedom, but when you ask them why they want that freedom, everything changes because it's then that they start thinking about their purpose.

Karen Auld,[20] a coach and consultant, told me about one of her clients, a franchisee who was working in a business that he didn't really like. His heart just wasn't in it. She knew that he'd taken on the franchise because he wanted freedom, but it wasn't until she asked him why he wanted that freedom that he really thought about it.

---

20. KCA website, www.karenauld.com/meet-karen, accessed 27 April 2022

Ultimately, he wanted the freedom because he wanted to buy the local football club in Italy, where he grew up. Thinking about this led him to realise what his first purpose was: he wanted to maximise financial freedom for his family, but his bigger purpose was to buy the club because of the way the it had motivated him as a child to be a better version of himself. He wanted to continue the local club so it inspired and trained young kids into the future.

A lot of people get stuck at a certain level and can't push beyond where they are because they haven't uncovered their true purpose. Purpose always goes beyond making money, and usually once people figure this out, they can push through to the next level and get behind something that's bigger than they are.

This is why it's important to have a purpose that's bigger than you are, and to build a business that's aligned with this purpose. Only then will you stay motivated enough to create a business that is truly sustainable.

TOP TIPS FOR FINDING YOUR PURPOSE

1. Identify your stakeholders. Most businesses have owners, employees, clients, shareholders, etc, but the great businesses see that the planet is also a stakeholder. Remember not to take your eye off the bottom line, though. If you're not profitable, you're not going to be able to look after any of your stakeholders.

2. Ask yourself 'Why?' Why are you truly doing what you're doing? As mentioned, most entrepreneurs start with wanting freedom, but their real purpose is deeper than this. Why do you want freedom? What do you want to do with the money you make?

3. Go back into your childhood. Often something in your childhood will have influenced the way you see the world. Ask yourself the deep questions about your motivations. Once you understand the core reason behind your drive to do what you're doing, everything else will fall into place.

4. Find the tingle. Look for the emotion that sparks your fire. What gave you that first tingle that made you want to move forward? Where do you find your joy? See if you can translate that into what you're doing on an everyday basis because it's that which will give you purpose. When was the first time you really felt as though you were making a difference? When what you were doing was bigger than you?

5. Imagine you're financially free and don't have to work. What will you do next? What will you invest in? What will you sink your teeth into? What will keep you busy? Answering these questions will help you find your purpose.

FIND YOUR FREEDOM

Set personal goals that require cash and time but will give you personal freedom – for example, having the time to take enough holidays with your family, teaching your kids to ski, seeing them in school plays, being able to spend quality time with your family; or to have the time to learn new skills, or to help other entrepreneurs or, even better, to have these and also have the ability to drive towards a bigger goal, such as making the planet better.

Summary

You'll only grow a successful and sustainable business if you know what your purpose is. Your purpose goes deeper than simply being passionate about something or having certain principles. When you uncover your purpose everything else falls into place, so it's important to spend time doing this.

In the next chapter, I'll talk about how to grow your success once you've discovered your purpose.

EIGHT

Refresh, Research, Repeat

In the last chapter, we examined how important purpose is to a business. Without a clear purpose, you won't be able to push through when times are tough.

In this chapter, I'm going to talk about why the three Rs – refresh, research and repeat – are necessary to grow a business.

Refresh

The Buddhist term *'shoshin'* means 'beginner's mind'. *Shoshin* requires you to come to a situation just as a beginner would, with an open mind, even if you have an advanced level of experience with the subject.[21]

---

21. Jarvie, J, 'Embracing *shoshin* – the beginner's mind', Medium (13 January 2021), https://jackjarvie.medium.com/embracing-shoshin -the-beginners-mind-f558d9c0e0e3, accessed 24 March 2022

I often go back to things that I looked at three or four years ago and apply the beginner's mind. I ask myself how I would approach the situation if it were brand new to me. We often develop blind spots, mainly due to limitations at the time, either the technology isn't there, or we didn't know what we know now about the area, or that it isn't the right time to implement those, and they get left behind, or remain blind spots. Returning to the beginner's mind can clear these spots.

Often the first time we come up against a problem we can't fix it because the technology doesn't exist or the resources aren't available. Because the problem can't be solved it's left, and after a while we get used to it and stop seeing that it's there. By the time you go back with a beginner's mind, though, there may be solutions.

This idea is similar to that of looking at things from a customer's perspective. Both approaches require you to step outside the way you always look at things and refresh your mind. Doing so will enable you to identify issues and resolve them.

Research

Research should be experimental. In marketing, for example, new channels are coming out almost daily, and it's about finding the best ROI on that. In terms of research, you need to look specifically at two things: marketing and technology.

Marketing: because this changes constantly Google launch new advertising products quite often, and being first to utilise them can get you a competitive advantage. Technology to drive operational efficiency and reduce costs or gain competitive advantage on partnerships.

In the middle of the courtyard at Google's headquarters there's a dinosaur to remind everyone that even the biggest, fiercest thing will die out if they don't adapt.[22] It's the constant play with research that keeps businesses alive.

Research is vital, but don't get caught in the trap of analysis. You can analyse forever. You can analyse the analysis, and then analyse the methodology of the analysis. If you're not careful, the analysis itself becomes the process. If you analyse everything, you don't do anything and you get stuck in a rut that you can't get out of.

Research, on the other hand, is about action, moving forward and trying new things. Research without implementation is a waste of time, so make sure that you put your research to good use and act on the information you uncover. The aim of your research is always

---

22. Coats, K, 'A lesson & warning from Stan the Dinosaur, *Tomorrow Today*, https://tomorrowtodayglobal.com/2011/01/04/a-lesson -warning-from-stan-the-dinosaur, accessed 22 April 2022

innovation, which is what makes a business stand out among its competitors.

If Henry Ford had looked at what people wanted, he would have given them a faster horse. Instead, he invented the car. He gave them something they didn't even know they wanted. The car is now a must-have for most people and is synonymous with personal freedom. Ford innovated. If he'd spent all his time doing the research and then analysing the research, he never would have invented the car – you also need to look outwards to innovate.

Going back to the idea of purpose for a moment: Ford was successful because he was driven by a purpose, a dream to make things better. His purpose was to make automobiles affordable.[23] His purpose was bigger than just an idea, bigger than a passion.

How franchising supports research and development

If you're a small business, you might not have the funds to do the research and development necessary to grow your business. The good thing about franchises is that it's done for you.

---

23. PBS, Who Made America: Henry Ford, www.pbs.org/wgbh /theymadeamerica/whomade/ford_hi.html, accessed 27 April 2022

The franchisor will complete the research needed to expand the franchise. Franchisees can access this research to develop their own businesses without having to carry it out themselves.

A good example of this is an experience I had with Fantastic Services pest control. We had a small franchise in the UK and were using familiar methods to control pests. In the UK, though, we don't have that many types of pest, so we don't have a lot of knowledge about the different methods available to control them.

When we saw how our franchisee in Australia was doing pest control, we had a light-bulb moment and quickly adopted the methods being used over there. Pests are much more of a problem in Australia than in the UK, so understandably, Australian pest controllers know a lot more about dealing with them. Our Australian franchisee's experience allowed us to grow our UK franchise with methods that other pest-control companies weren't aware of. This gave us an edge over our competitors.

The example links back to having a beginner's mind. We'd become stuck in our ways, and it wasn't until we took a different perspective and considered what we could learn from Australia that we were able to improve our processes and achieve innovation.

Franchising encourages you to think outside the box and to ask people questions, whereas with a start-up you'll likely see everyone else as a competitor. With franchising, you have access to more minds. Not all the ideas will be good ones, of course, but ideas will be generated. As well, people will be asking the questions that need to be answered to overcome problems and grow the business. Franchising and research go hand in hand, and the great thing about the franchise model is that everyone supports the research and benefits from it.

Growing through research

> 'Because the purpose of a business is to create a customer, the business enterprise has two – and only two – basic functions: marketing and innovation.'
> — Peter Drucker[24]

A lot of companies don't invest in research and development, and I don't believe that you can have innovation without it. And without innovation, you can't scale.

Peter Drucker's words are still relevant today. The successful companies are the ones that evolve, and research is the thing that helps them to do so. When a business owner looks at things with a beginner's mind and understands how important research is, they can take their business from being just a company in their sector to being a leader in their sector.

---

24. Forbes, 'Peter Drucker on Marketing', *Forbes* (3 July 2006), www .forbes.com/2006/06/30/jack-trout-on-marketing-cx_jt_0703drucker .html?sh=9b18fe2555cb, accessed 24 March 2022

Research is the brain of the company, and purpose is the heart.

Some parts of your business will not improve

When we were scaling Fantastic Services and applied a beginner's mind, we always saw room for improvement. It's also important to realise, though, that some parts of the business will never improve and that other parts aren't worth improving. To find out which areas of your business are worth spending this time and energy on, use a principle called ICE.

The ICE principle was coined by Sean Ellis and is an adapted model used by car manufacturing to determine which parts of the business to focus on developing. ICE stands for impact, confidence and ease and the idea behind it is that when a business is looking at innovating, it needs to focus on the things that result in a high impact but require low cost and effort to achieve.[25]

If you can find an area of the business where ICE can be applied, that's the golden nugget to explore. It's about identifying what impact your research will have – because there's no point researching something that's not going to have an impact.

---

25. Sergeev, A, 'How ICE score method helps to choose better product features' (28 August 2018), https://hygger.io/blog/ice-method-helps -choose-better-product-features, accessed 27 April 2022

Repeat

It's believed Bruce Lee had a saying that he's not afraid of a man who's practised a thousand kicks but of a man who's practised the same kick a thousand times. In business it's the same. If you are going to beat competition on a particular field, you have to find the method that is the most efficient. This can be by trial and error, but if you can find a person who has done it 1,000 times, then they are more likely to succeed.

Real mastery comes through repetition. In *Outliers*, Malcolm Gladwell talks about how mastery requires doing something for 10,000 hours.[26] You don't become a master overnight. You become a master by consistently doing the same things – over and over and over again.

Think of it like going to the gym. You build muscle through repetition. The number of reps you do is more important than the number of exercises. This is what Bruce Lee recognised.

Repetition with franchising

As a business model, franchising scores so highly in so many different areas because it's all about repetition. That's what franchises do – they repeat success over and over, across multiple locations (often across different

---

26. Gladwell, M, *Outliers: The story of success* (Penguin, 2009)

countries). Repetition is at the core of the franchise business model.

If you're a franchisee, you know exactly what model works best, and you know exactly what you need to do to achieve success. Then you repeat that success, again and again.

The Beatles produced a lot of albums – they were like a song factory. They understood what worked, they had a process they followed and they repeated their success. With that understanding, they mixed this with research into new sounds and ways of producing, like using stereo recordings, to remain fresh and ahead. This is why they're the most successful band of all time. They're a great example of how repeating a proven process leads to success.

TOP TIPS FOR REFRESHING, RESEARCHING AND REPEATING

1. **If you're not growing, refresh.** Go back to the problem with a beginner's mind. Use *shoshin* to put you in a better state to think about your business, your processes, a project, or a problem.

2. **Repeat, repeat, repeat.** If you're having success with something, keep investing in that and repeat the success over and over again. Keep doing the things that work.

3. **Measure twice, cut once.** Carry out all the research that's required before making a decision. Better to

wait and be sure than to jump in and realise later that you've made a costly mistake because you didn't have all the data needed to make an informed decision. You also need to make sure that you're researching the right things. Remember ICE. Look for solutions that have a high impact but involve low cost and low effort.

4. **Don't be difficult.** Try to be popular. Remember the Beatles and the success that they had in refreshing the things that were popular. Popularity is reached by repeating and improving what's already a success.

5. **'Steal like an artist.'** Austin Kleon says that you have to steal like an artist. There are good and bad ways to steal. Good theft is when you use other people's ideas to further your development but honour the people that you're inspired by. Always give them credit and add something of your own to the mix. You need to transform their ideas, or remix things so that you're adding something valuable.

Bad theft is when you degrade another person's ideas by copying them without credit and without adding anything to them. It's good to be inspired – just make sure you give credit where it's due.[27]

Summary

To grow your business, refresh, research and repeat. If you do each of these things consistently, you'll find it much easier to scale your business. Learn from what

27. Kleon, A, *Steal Like an Artist: 10 things nobody told you about being creative* (Workman, 2012)

the franchises do. Research and then distribute the outcomes of this research throughout your business.

In the next chapter, I'm going to inspire you about systems.

NINE

Systems

In the last chapter, I talked about how important it is to refresh, research and repeat. Another important thing to consider when growing your business, especially from a start-up, is which type of systems you need to implement to support your growth.

In this chapter, I'm going to explain why systems are so valuable and help you to understand when to implement them.

Systems set you free

the time Fantastic Services was launched, a few of our competitors were rushing into building systems, automating services and developing minimum viable products. For us, it was much simpler because we couldn't afford to build the big systems that we have today. We used Google Docs for the first year that we were in business, and I remember sitting with a member of staff who happens to be with us to this day, and who was struggling to open the daily schedule because the number of clients had increased so much that the database was taking longer and longer to load and it couldn't be solved by adding more memory to the computer, this meant we knew we had a hit!

Unlike our competitors, we didn't jump into developing systems because we knew that first we had to work out what was needed. We built our business the lean way. We started with one Google Sheet for the month. When a client called, or emailed or completed the booking form, the sheet grew bigger and bigger and we had to shift to a weekly one. Then the number of rows on the sheet ran out and the memory on our computers had to be upgraded.

It was time to implement the first system, which we called Cleaning CRM. It was basic but became the foundation for something much, much bigger. It allowed us to run any service or product on-demand and eventually meant that we could show real-time availability, which none of our competitors was able to do.

Before we went down the route of building systems, though, we had to decide whether to build or buy. We looked at numerous systems. Some were able to take the bookings, others could handle the scheduling and others could provide the call centre function, but nothing suited Fantastic Services completely. There was no system out there that could show availability and the customised price, book the service and then take customers through a checkout service in which they could pay for add-ons.

The need to automate

Most of the systems we looked at were either basic or had a single function. What we needed for Fantastic Services was much more advanced – something that could truly allow us to become the best place to book and get services. We mapped out the processes that we needed to replace and thought about how we would get our clients, pros and franchisees on board. We didn't just want to replace paper with systems – we wanted to leapfrog the whole thing and automate, as this would be the most efficient way to grow the business.

Because we were so deep into our operations and had mapped every single process, we had a clear idea of how to automate. We began with the end in mind and knew that we wanted to become a platform where you could add any service with any skill and make it bookable online while also automating the back end so that when a booking was made, it was automatically added to the schedule.

We wanted to include all the services that we offered, even if it became a partner company who performed them. We wanted to become the marketplace where any service anywhere could be booked. Imagine if you booked a gardening service but could then add waste removals so that two or three separate bookings became one! Our goal was to productise our services, and although we knew that this was an enormous task, to this day, we're still a leader in it. Cleaning CRM became the foundation for what is now a fully fledged automation software company called serviceOS.com which from being a Customer Relations Managment sytem, became the operating system for a service company.

Most software focuses on single vertical businesses, whereas Fantastic Services is a multi-skill business with more than sixty services, from cleaning to pest control and now beauty and wellness.

We couldn't have done this without automation, and without funding serviceOS as a platform.

Performance visibility

When the idea for our unique operating system was born, we needed to ensure we found someone who could make it happen with full visibility by making our systems show our results on daily operations and our financial performance and quality. I started searching and found Milen Hristov, who became our chief technology officer. Milen shared our belief in the importance of using systems and technology where you can and people where it matters.

We knew that some things are done better by people and that something has added value if performed by a human rather than a machine. Anything that has to be done more than three times must become a system, though. When we were growing we found that some processes became standard practices. When we implemented a new practice, we made the rule that if it had to be done more than three times, and had to be replicated for scale, it must become a system process. An example was adding invoices or when an invoice was updated manually, we needed to ensure it was reflected it in the system. Milen came from the travel industry and had lots of experience creating packages, which was useful to us at Fantastic Services.

At the time of writing, ServiceOS.com handles 100,000 jobs daily and is the operating system used in several start-ups, as well as established service companies across the globe.

The principles we learned on the journey were different from those I'd learned in my early years as a systems engineer and product designer. I saw that the 'one size fits all' approach didn't fit systems that became too big to manage. A 'try first, build once' method was much better.

Creating systems

Here are six things to consider when building a system.

1. **Start with a minimum viable product.** Fake the flow until you know what you need then test it and let it run. You might start with an analogue version, or use spreadsheets.

2. **Source ideas.** It's easy to create a process and automate it, but you need to make sure you're automating the right thing. I've seen so many dashboards that look pretty but only replicate an old process which doesn't require new systems. Also remember that those shiny dashboards require someone to watch them. How much better would it be to create an automated process or system that looked after itself?

3. **Only fix it if it's worth it.** At Fantastic Services, we knew that we had a lot of areas that needed improvement. Big companies often build their way out of problems, but we didn't have the budget to do this. Instead, we had to carefully consider what we wanted to do. We'd try things out before building the system, and we'd build it only if it fixed the problem that we wanted to solve. This mentality helped us avoid going down the rabbit hole of building for the sake of building. We could quickly see the impact something would have before building the feature. Even now, we keep trying things, and if

something is worth designing, we make it fast as we know exactly what it's supposed to do.

4. **Get close.** Our IT team sat next to our service development team for a reason. Mixing up the teams allows us to get to know each other better as people and also helps us to understand the business needs of each team. Often the business developer sits in a bubble and doesn't meet the clients or the end users, but to make a product better, you need to understand it from all angles. One of the ways we do this is by having our teams sit close to each other. We even went as far as sending our developers on cleaning jobs with the pros so they could really understand the problems faced on a daily basis

5. **Don't build a faster horse.** In the previous chapter, we looked at Henry Ford, who designed a car instead of a faster horse, which was what people would have wanted at the time. Sometimes it's best to not give the people what they want and give them something better. Always look closely at the end goal and think about the best way to reach it. Our end goal was to create a service that people loved, technology that made things simpler and a business that put people first. We had to think as owners and product designers as well as end users. We had to return to a beginner's mind to figure out what was needed. In a world that constantly demands better systems, you have to anticipate the

adaptation of technology. Back when we started, we were told that it would be impossible to get a cleaner by selecting the job online and then editing the job to suit your preferences. Now, years later, it happens more than 200 times a day. My experience in mobile phone games in 1999 came in handy here. Experience had taught me that adaptation would grow exponentially. When we applied this thinking to Fantastic Services, we didn't just make one change – we made rocket-ship moves. We didn't just change how the system worked – we reinvented how the service operated.

6. **Explore before you build or buy.** I can't tell you how to pick a system for your industry, or how many platforms you should have, but I can tell you that you need to think about what you want. Some booking platforms are so generic that you'll have problems making anything work on them. A system should, first and foremost, serve the basic needs of the business, but it should also have the potential to grow with your company. You don't want to customise it too much because as you grow, you'll want to change things.

As Fantastic Services has grown and we've started to serve larger and larger clients, our system has developed into an operating system from a single-service platform. We built it to be able to book anything anywhere, and it's become the system of choice for service companies. I'm proud that the little engine we built inside Fantastic Services as spreadsheets in the beginning, are now the backbone in companies globally, and growing on a daily basis.

You need to consider long-term what matters in a system. Before you build, though, look at the problem at hand. Is the solution replicable? It might involve payroll, rescheduling or reminders, but if it's replicable, it's possible to automate. The question to ask yourself is this: 'If I double my sales and my clients, will my costs also double?' If the answer is yes, you need a system that will enable you to grow.

Summary

Before you embark on the journey of building your own system, many companies can do this, but you need to do your research on software for your industry. In most cases you can choose between simple systems or more advanced systems, like serviceOS.com, but if you go down the route of developing, keep the simple principles in mind: start with an MVP, test it before you embark, play it out on paper, on no code and be stringent with development. Franchising is a whole different model on its own, and there are many companies providing software for the franchise industry, but very often they miss out on the mix between franchisee and franchisor and doesn't take the client into consideration. Software that's built for the consumer world often doesn't work in the world of franchise.

TEN

Optimise

In the last chapter, I discussed why systems are critical to the success of your business.

In this chapter, I'm going to talk about how to optimise your business by making your systems and processes as efficient as possible.

Don't 'go lean' on people

Profit is the result of how well you run your business. When you know what it costs to acquire employees or customers and you're managing sales the way you're supposed to, you'll likely be rewarded by profit.

The way to optimise your business is to take some of that profit and put it back into the business. Use it to improve your systems and processes and make your business more efficient.

I run my business on the belief that you should never spend as much money as you think you should. You need to think carefully about your business needs – don't spend money just because you have it to spend. Before making a purchase, ask yourself, 'Is this a real business need or a nice-to-have?' Never spend money if it's not a need. This doesn't mean you shouldn't invest in something that's expensive. For example, consultants are expensive, but they can also be invaluable if you're hiring them for the right purpose.

In franchises, a lot of the investment decisions are easier because the owner will have ideas about where you should invest your profits. You can also share some of those costs with your peers, the other franchisees, for example if you can get a deal on equipment or suppliers. There's also more you can do in a franchise to optimise costs than in any other type of business because, as I've said, franchises are built on repeated success.

I spoke to Erik Van Horn, founder of Mighty Dog Franchises in the US, who said that the most important thing to remember when optimising was not to 'go lean' on your people. When you're starting out, the first couple of people you recruit will hopefully go on to become the managers of your business further down the line – so it's really important that you don't skimp on your people. Make sure that they're a good fit for your business and spend money training them properly. When you're thinking about where to reinvest your profits, your people should always be at the top of your list.

There are certain functions that you don't need every day, say a head of international franchising or a CFO, for example. Instead of having them on your permanent payroll, hire them to work for you virtually a couple of days a month. You can spend the money you save on their salaries on other areas of the business.

Optimising vs maximising

Optimising and maximising are different, so you need to think about them in different ways.

Optimising is about what goes on behind the scenes, and maximising is what happens when you're scaling. You need to know whether you're in the optimising or the maximising phase of your business because you can't do both at once.

Optimising involves looking at your processes and systems and seeing what you can cut back on, or streamline. It's about making your business leaner and more efficient. You might not always save money by optimising, but you will lay the foundations which will enable your business to scale. Maximising involves growing your business fast and taking it to the next level.

We'll take a closer look at maximising in Chapter 12.

Marketing

In regards to marketing, when you're maximising, the cost per acquisition should be lower than the lifetime value of a customer, meaning the cost of getting a client should be less than the lifetime profits of a client. When you're growing your business, though, you've also got to understand that the lifetime value isn't complete yet, which means that you should expect your cost per acquisition to increase. The best thing that you can do with your marketing when you're maximising is to measure your return on investment and set specific goals regarding the number of customers you should have and how much you're willing to spend to get them.

When you're maximising, consider investing until you reach critical mass – ie the product or service is so high in the customer's mind that it grows on autopilot.

Optimising your marketing is about prioritising what to do first. There's no point jumping straight to the costly options (eg TV or radio advertising). When you optimise your marketing, take a good look at your business and think about the outcomes you want – then try to achieve them without spending all your money.

There are several things you can do at a grassroots level to grow your business. The best place to start depends on your industry, and again where your customers find you. It can be by increasing your SEO ranking, it can be growing your followers on Instagram or raising your Linkedin profile, or appearing in every directory where people search for your type of business. It really does depend on where your clients are, and what type of business you are in. You need to find out what's the most effective channel for your business.

Another efficient way to grow your business is with Google AdWords. Google has mastered the business of response marketing, so if you invest in this, you'll most likely see a return on your investment. Google AdWords is effective because people usually intend to make a purchase when they search Google for a business in their area. If your business is at the top of the results page, there's a good chance you'll gain the customer.

The next best thing is to increase your social media presence and your online visibility. You do this by being more active on the channels you use and by using multiple platforms.

Another way to grow is to get involved in your community. You could sponsor local projects to get PR opportunities on TV and radio. Paying for national media coverage should be last on your list because it's expensive and only now it's getting more targeted, but it also comes with a lot of budgets and risk.

The type of business you have will determine the types of marketing activities you engage in, but you should always start with the cheapest thing on your list and build from there.

Once a business has more than one or two employees, divide the responsibilities: one person focusing on optimising and the other on maximising. You'll have one person whose job it is to sell, sell, sell and do more and more marketing, while the other person will make sure you don't lose sales or customers.

Focus on the things that bring in the money

In his book *The Pumpkin Plan*, Mike Michalowicz uses the analogy of a pumpkin field to explain what you should focus on in a business. He describes a field full of pumpkins that are exactly the same as each other except for one, which stands out because it's huge. Michalowicz says we should spend our time and resources figuring out how the pumpkin got so big and then replicating that process.[28]

Figuring out what makes the pumpkin grow and then repeating that is what's going to help you to optimise and then maximise. Nothing else will.

---

28. Michalowicz, M, *The Pumpkin Plan: A simple strategy to grow a remarkable business in any field* (Portfolio, 2012)

It's important to not get distracted. Once you know what grows the pumpkin (profit), focus your energy on it instead of trying to do a million other things. Securing that profit means that you'll have money to invest in the next step.

Optimising is about focusing on growing that one big pumpkin that's going to feed everyone and bring in the money that will enable you to grow other parts of your business. Know where your money is coming from and understand what makes you profitable. You need to go really deep on that.

Entrepreneurs tend to get distracted because they want to create and move on to the next thing. It's easy to lose focus on the things that matter, so make sure you don't take your eye off the pumpkin. It's profit that feeds your dreams. Cultivate a narrow mind about this.

Optimisation will benefit your business

Nowadays, with advances in technology, almost every process in your business can be automated, which means that optimisation is easy.

Booking and rescheduling processes, customer complaint and feedback handling, invoicing, fulfilment, and service delivery can all be automated. Even most marketing functions can be optimised. Every couple of months there's new software to help automate processes, so there's really no excuse for not optimising things.

In the early days of a business, the founder or owner will likely perform every business function themselves, so things will naturally be optimised. As the business grows, the owner will need to decide which functions they want to keep doing and which ones they will outsource or employ someone to do.

As mentioned earlier, if there's something you're not good at, instead of wasting time trying to become good at it, it's better to get someone else to do it. That's how you begin to optimise for the long-term.

The impact of optimising

When I consider projects with a view to optimising, I always look at the impact that optimising will have on the business. I consider the ROI and use the ICE methodology that I talked about in Chapter 8. The idea is to measure the investment against the impact and the cost and effort involved in getting there.

Ultimately, optimising should free you up to focus on other things. If you're spending too much time and energy on recruitment, for example, it could be that you're missing out on the high-impact outcome of winning a big corporate deal.

Sometimes the cost of optimisation is high but the impact is exponential. For example, the cost of building software, as we did at Fantastic Services, is high and the effort required to build it was tremendous. The impact of building it was huge, though, because we could suddenly scale the business.

With franchises, it's even easier to work out what to optimise because the franchisor will tell you. Ask them what will have the biggest impact on recruitment, sales, marketing or reducing costs. You can find out exactly how much effort X, Y or Z is going to take because someone will already have done it and you can learn from their experiences.

Identifying areas of improvement

When I'm looking at whether to optimise, I go into every department within my business and ask myself, 'If I double clients, sales or recruitment tomorrow, will the cost of this department also double?'

If you can double your sales without doubling the cost of running a department, then you've got something scalable. If not, you need to look at your processes in that department and improve them.

This is a simple methodology, and it works every single time.

Not everything will have an impact

Not everything that you do will have a direct impact, or the impact you wanted. It was like this at Fantastic

Services when we looked into the problem of people arriving late to their jobs. At first we tried to optimise everything regarding travel time, but nothing made a difference. There was no impact.

It wasn't until we started measuring the right thing – whether they were on time for their first jobs – that we saw an impact on the business. Keep this in mind when you think about optimising. Work out the things that you think will have the most impact, but don't be surprised if your optimisation doesn't give you the results you expect.

Reducing costs

Optimising is also about reducing business costs. Regular costs are the ones you need to focus on because as your business grows, these will increase. Salaries, equipment and running costs can add up to a huge amount, so it's important to work out how and where you can cut costs. As I said earlier, it's often a good idea to hire someone on a temporary basis to manage a project or complete a process than to recruit somebody to work for you full time.

If you look at your costs with a beginner's mind, you might be surprised at how much money you can save by finding different ways of doing things. Is everything that you spend money on strictly necessary? Or can some spending be reduced or stopped altogether?

One of the key things to look at is your sales formula. What is the cost of each acquisition (ie what are your marketing costs) and what is the conversion rate? How many leads are your salespeople converting? Every single time you increase your percentages in conversion, or decrease cancellations, you decrease the cost per acquisition, and this means that your conversion rates go up.

If you're looking at your business and think that the cost per acquisition is high, it's crucial to figure out what you can do inside the sales funnel to improve things. I've often seen people with decent-sized budgets not measuring what goes on further down the line in the sales process. Because of their budget, they feel they don't need to worry about that. This is a mistake, though. Always keep an eye on your costs per acquisition because if you can optimise things and increase your percentages, your business will become much more profitable.

TOP TIPS FOR OPTIMISATION

1. **Monitor the ROI of your marketing spend.** In the scaling phase you can't expect the cost per acquisition to be lower than the lifetime value, but you should consistently try to improve the ROI through optimisation. For example, with franchising, make sure your franchisee recruitment is optimised.

2. **Remember that sales can always be improved.** You need to look at your sales funnel regularly to see what can be optimised to make things better.

3. **Don't go lean on your staff.** Don't hire staff members for the sake of having them, either.

4. **Make sure that you're spending money only on the things that matter.** Always ask, do I really need this or is it a 'nice to have'?

5. **Automate.** The more you can automate, the more you're going to save in the long-term. See what tools are out there and use them.

FIND THE RIGHT SUPPLIERS

Review your suppliers and make sure they're fit for purpose and will support your growth.

Summary

Hopefully it's clear how important it is to optimise your business, and the steps you need to take to do so.

In the next chapter, I'm going to talk about three bigger-picture concepts to consider in any business: happiness, hard work and health.

ELEVEN

Happiness, Hard Work And Health

In the last chapter, I explained what it means to optimise your business and described the best ways of doing this.

In this chapter, I'm going to talk about three fundamental concepts to incorporate into any business: happiness, hard work and health.

Happiness isn't a destination

Dr Robert Holden is a British psychologist who has studied the psychology of happiness, and is a good friend of mine.[29] His work involves coaching on what

29. Holden, R, www.robertholden.com, accessed 27 April 2022

makes people happy, and he argues that happiness isn't a destination but a frequency. He asks us to imagine it's like a radio station you tune to.

Culturally, we tend to think that happiness is something we'll arrive at in the future. We believe that when we buy that car or that house or make seven figures, for example, we'll feel happy, so we see happiness as a goal to achieve rather than an important part of our lives now – but goals have little to do with happiness.

Happiness is about creating harmony in your work so that you can reach your definition of success. Success is about much more than money. Robert emphasises that you have to understand what happiness truly means to you. Once you do, you can find ways to incorporate it into your everyday life.

What does success mean to you?

Dr Holden's research ties in with my ideas about success. When you take the time to think about what success really means to you, and realise that it's not all about hitting financial goals, you'll find it much easier to change things in your life to help you to achieve it.

You need to define success in a more personal way. I always say that it's okay to not have a billion-dollar company if it's a company that you're proud of and that has a culture of respect, if it's a company that gives you satisfaction and joy and, most importantly, lets you fulfil a purpose.

Success might look like having more time to spend with your family, or having less stress in your life. Again, it's important to define success in the way that you want to, but if it doesn't include things that make you happy, you probably need to rewrite your definition.

Hard work: Rethink the hustle

For years, the entrepreneurial community has been taught to think that business is about hustling and working eighty-hour weeks. This doesn't have to be the case. Outsourcing and hiring the right people is a much better, and smarter, way to work. If you're not careful, hustling can kill you.

Of course you have to put in the hours and work hard, and at times it might seem like an uphill battle, but if you work smart and have the best people helping you, things will get easier and eventually, the ball will roll down the hill at a high speed.

Seth Godin wrote a book called *The Dip*, which offers an interesting analysis of when to stick at something and when to quit. He explains that if you're in a hole trying to push a ball up, you should quit but if you are trying to push a ball up a hill, the ball will gain automatic momentum, start rolling on its own, so you should stick with it. [30] So if in business you're going up a hill and the ball gets momentum, which means you'll reach critical mass in your business, then you should stick. If you're smart, you'll employ salespeople, and other professionals to help you grow the business as you're rolling the ball up the hill. This will help you gain the momentum that will get you over the top.

Ask yourself, 'Is the hard work getting me over the top of the mountain or is it just getting me out of a hole?' Your answer will determine whether you should stick or quit.

Free yourself

Not many jobs give you equity. It's rare for employees to be rewarded when the company that they work for does well, and there's also no guarantee that the company will be functioning in ten years. We all know how it goes in business. I once held valuable shares in a telecoms company that are now worth nothing.

When you work as an employee, you can get stuck in 'dead man's shoes', which means that to progress, somebody above you has to leave or retire. Unless the company is growing rapidly, you'll always be stuck, and if you're not careful, you can end up becoming institutionalised.

---

30. Godin, S, *The Dip: A little book that teaches you when to quit (and when to stick)* (Portfolio, 2007)

The only real way to be free in your career is to be in charge of your own destiny – by running a start-up, buying a company or investing in a franchise. As Robert Kiyosaki says, the whole goal is to make money work for you, not for you to work for money.[31]

It's important not to misunderstand the word 'freedom'. It's not necessarily about being free financially. When you run your own business, you can choose whether to work hard or not. If you're at a time in your life when you can't work hard, or you can't take risks, you won't grow the business and you won't make as much money, but you'll be less stressed. That's freedom – the ability to choose when and how to work.

One of the great things about franchises is that you have much more flexibility regarding downtime. If you want, you can spend two or three years working very hard and then have a couple of years where you don't work as hard. The franchise model supports this way of working. It's much more flexible than a start-up because the systems and processes that need to be followed to grow the business are in place. You can decide where and when you're going to invest your time and energy.

---

31. Kiyosaki, R, 'The rich vs the poor when it comes to investing time' (26 October 2021), www.richdad.com/rich-vs-poor, accessed 27 April 2022

Franchise work pays off

It can be amazing to build and grow a start-up, and there's potentially a big exit. You put in the hard work, build up your equity and your assets in the business and then eventually you can sell it, sometimes for a life-changing amount of money.

The unfortunate fact is that most start-ups fail. The list of reasons is endless. The failure can be due to personal circumstances, environmental factors, economic reasons, competitors or even a lack of understanding of the business.

Buying into a business is kind of the same. Unless the founder is still there driving things, you'll end up with a brand and a name but not necessarily a business. In many cases, you'll have to put more money into the business after you've bought it. Unless you've got everything worked out, you could end up losing a lot.

This is what makes a franchise such a good investment. Of course there's no guarantee that you'll do well, and you'll still have to put in the work. It's not going to grow automatically, and it's most definitely not a get-rich-quick scheme. If you're not a salesperson, you've got to hire one. If you're not the best person at operations management, you've got to hire that person. These people will cost you money. If you're looking at what you can spend your time on wisely over a decade, though, a franchise is always going to be better than a start-up or an existing business because it's got a much higher chance of success.

You also have the potential to exit the business and make money when you sell it. You might not make as much as you would from selling a start-up, but with the start-up you have to build assets, like brand value, technology and processes that are worth more than just the number of clients you have.

As mentioned, because franchises are proven business models with many successful case studies to draw from, getting the funding you need to get things off the ground will be easier. The financing will also be different. With a start-up, you'll likely have an investor who'll end up owning part of your company. Your share will go down every time someone puts money in. This isn't the case with a franchise. With a franchise you can make a smaller investment as a lot of the investment is created by the franchisor – making the product or the service, building up the brand recognition, systems and technology and the training, you get all this plus the learning from mistakes, at a fraction of the cost compared to learning by doing.

The Wheel of Growth

To help make the hard work not as hard, I've developed a shortcut that will help you get the results you want for your business without having to learn through trial and error. The shortcut comes from my experiences with franchises, but it can be applied to any business. I was inspired by Jim Collins's flywheel concept, which helps you to identify the big things that will help your company grow.[32]

There are many parts to the Wheel of Growth. At Fantastic Services, we know how important it is to focus on all of them in steps and to continue to come back to them to grow the business.

1. Attract the right people. Employing the wrong people will harm you in the long run.

2. Consistently deliver quality so that your customers come back.

3. Be excellent at marketing, or bring on board marketing experts, to reduce your cost per acquisition.

4. Automate all the processes that you can to cut costs.

5. Expand into new areas. This might mean going into new geographical territories or adding to your services and products.

6. Become an influencing authority, a source of inspiration within your sector.

7. Repeat.

---

32. Collins, J, 'The Flywheel Effect', www.jimcollins.com/concepts/the
-flywheel.html, accessed 24 March 2022

By taking these principles on board, you'll really start to understand your business and how easy it is to grow, regardless of whether it's a franchise or a start-up.

You might want to adapt the Wheel of Growth that we use to make it more relevant to your business.

Following the method laid out in the Wheel of Growth will help to eliminate some of the hard work and hopefully give you more time to tap into your happiness.

Don't be afraid of hard work

In every business, there will be times when things get tough. It's the businesses that keep on going no matter how difficult it gets that are successful, though.

Remember your purpose. It will help you keep going in the tough times, which is why uncovering and understanding it early on is so important. If you've got a strong purpose and a clear vision, it's much easier to bounce back from the disasters and keep moving forwards.

It takes courage, commitment and hard work to create anything of value. Don't give up too easily. Use the Wheel of Growth to help you identify what you need to focus on and then put your head down and work hard to get to where you want to be.

Health and happiness

In his book *The Hard Thing About Hard Things*, Ben Horowitz writes that in a start-up, you'll find two emotions, euphoria and terror, and that lack of sleep enhances them both.[33]

Becoming an entrepreneur is a quest for freedom. It's about being your own boss, about being in charge of your destiny. When you get wins it creates a sense of euphoria. The difference between start-ups and franchises is that although you have the euphoria with both, running a franchise doesn't involve the same kind of terror – to use an earlier analogy, when you jump off the cliff, you don't need to assemble the airplane on the way down.

Whether you're a start-up or a franchisee, though, you need to make sure that you look after yourself on the journey. As Horowitz says, a lack of sleep makes the good times better and the bad times worse[34], so if you want to avoid the roller coaster of emotions associated with starting a new business, make sure you're getting enough sleep.

33. Horowitz, B, *The Hard Thing About Hard Things: Building a business when there are no easy answers* (HarperBus, 2014)
34. Horowitz, B, *The Hard Thing About Hard Things: Building a business when there are no easy answers* (HarperBus, 2014)

Life doesn't have to be a hustle

I've talked a lot about the things that you need to do to grow your business, but ultimately, all that really matters is your health and happiness. If you have an unhealthy relationship with your business because you're working all the time and not able to enjoy your business or your life in general, it's probably time to stop. If you're not sleeping and are shifting from euphoria to terror and back again, your mental health will suffer, and this is going to impact all parts of your life.

Keep Dr Holden's words in mind to live a healthy life. Happiness isn't a destination. It's not something that you should aspire to achieve in the future – it's something that you should be able to tap into all the time.

It's worth repeating: if you don't have your health and happiness, nothing else matters. There's no greater success than being healthy and happy. Don't get so caught up in growing your business that you forget that.

Summary

If you want to be truly successful in life, your happiness and health have to be at the heart of everything you do. It's important to grow your business and achieve your ambitions through hard work, but success isn't all about making money. It can be easy to forget that.

In the next chapter, I'm going to talk about maximising.

TWELVE
Maximise

In the last chapter, I discussed why the most important things in business, and in life, are to be happy and healthy. It's common to define success in terms of finances, but real success is about a lot more than money.

Happiness often involves freedom. When the money and the people are both working for you, and not the other way around, you find freedom. You get to this point by training and then scaling, or maximising, which is what we're going to look at in this chapter.

A different mindset

Maximising is a whole different ball game from optimising. At this point, you're looking to push your business. They're two sides of the same coin, though. If you haven't optimised, it's going to be impossible to maximise.

When you're optimising, you're figuring out how to make things smoother and cutting back on the unnecessary processes. When you're maximising, you're figuring out what you can do to grow the business and double or quadruple the amount of income coming in without doubling or quadrupling costs.

A couple of Harvard students are working together running hundreds of fast-food chains.[35] Even though they're young, they've created a highly successful business buying franchises, repeating their success and achieving proper economies of scale. This reveals how there's a whole other industry inside the franchising industry – successful multi-unit franchising. What these students know how to do is maximise, and if you really want to grow your business, you'll need to know how too.

The franchise model lends itself to maximising because the whole ecosystem supports growth. You build one franchise, and once you've reached a level of success with it and you're confident that you know what you need to do to repeat that success, you take on another

---

35. Reuter, D, 'How 4 Harvard grads built their empires franchising with brands like Wendy's, Taco Bell, Burger King, and Popeyes', *Insider* (29 August 2020), www.businessinsider.com/how-harvard-business -school-ivy-league-grads-fast-food-franchise-empires, accessed 27 April 2022

franchise. Scaling the next franchise will be even easier because you're simply compounding the successes of your first. This is what the students did with such impressive results.

The key is to understand the Wheel of Growth, which we looked at in the previous chapter, and find ways to make it run faster and bigger. Once you've figured that out, maximising is easy.

A true entrepreneur will keep putting money into the success formula and then look to scale it.

Maximising your business

Recruit well

Whether you have a franchise or a start-up, when it comes to maximising, the most important thing is to make sure that your first couple of recruits are really good. You need to plan for the long-term, and those first employees will likely be the ones who end up running the business. Make sure that the people you recruit in the beginning are good enough to run things two, three, four years down the line. You need to take a long-term view if you're serious about scaling.

Remember the importance of training, which we looked at in Chapter 6. When you help people get to know the business and understand their role and function within it, you lay a strong foundation for maximising.

Avoid skimming your company dry

I've seen a lot of people get to a point where their business is making six figures and then get distracted by the money and stop investing in the business, especially in the service industry. They stop investing in assets and in scale and instead start disinvesting in things such as property or cars.

A true entrepreneur knows that a six-figure business has huge potential to grow even more. A surprising number of business owners don't realise this, though, and instead of building, they start to skim their companies dry.

Reinvestment is key to growth, and when Anton and I founded Fantastic Services, we signed a formal agreement in which we committed to reinvesting 80% of the profits back into the business each year. We knew that we could create a successful company and that we'd probably reach the seven-figure mark quickly. We worried our focus on the business would decrease once we started making money above our salaries.

Keep Mike Michalowicz's pumpkin in mind. In business it's easy to get distracted and move from one thing to another, but this approach doesn't grow big pumpkins. Lay your foundation and focus. Along these lines, don't stray too far from what motivates you. When you focus on doing the things that align with your purpose, you'll see your pumpkins grow.

The agreement that Anton and I made allowed us to keep feeding the Wheel of Growth. If you don't do this, everything starts to fall off the wheel. A friend of mine came up with the phrase 'eat like a mouse, shit like an elephant', and this sums up my view on optimising, but when it comes to investing, take only the amount you need out of the business. Everything else goes back in to maximise.

Unless you're a monopoly, there's always room for growth. Many people reinvest too little in the business in the first couple of years, and this negatively affects their ability to scale. I know that 80% might seem enormous, but you can always reduce that number later, or you can just maximise your business until the 20% is in where you want it to be.

It's important to understand that if you've got a successful business model, to really reap the rewards, you have to focus on that and you have to invest in that – and with a franchise, unlike with a start-up, you have a well-trodden path to help you do that.

Do you have the capacity to scale?

Anton believes that once someone becomes a businessperson or an entrepreneur, they won't stay in one business. Most investigate other things they want to do, even if their first business gives them the biggest return. Once you've had a taste of running a business and creating something successful, you may find you want to go out and repeat that process somewhere else.

If you're doing something well, do it twice. Repetition is what it takes to maximise your return, but our nature as entrepreneurs is such that we'll seek different challenges despite the return. **To avoid the lure of differentiation, learn the principle of maximisation.** Fantastic Services offers multiple units and types of franchises. This helps us alleviate boredom and also achieve a compounding effect.

Before you scale, though, you have to ask yourself, your family and the people you trust whether you have the capacity to do it. Think carefully about the learning journey and the effort that will be necessary to scale your business. Be honest with yourself about your capacity – and ability. You'll save yourself a lot of time and money this way.

The franchise entrepreneurs who went from six to seven figures, such as the ones I interviewed for this book, were the ones who understood that they had to open another franchise to do it. They understood that they needed to reinvest to scale and were ready to have less income for a while and put it into growing the business. They had a long-term strategy in mind from the start.

The thing to remember is that you're serving a client, so at the end of the day, you've got to find out what your client wants to see if there's potential to scale. You might not have enough customers to make scaling possible.

Everything comes back to knowing your business, your clients and the market. Scaling won't always be the right thing to do.

Scaling franchises

Franchises are a lot easier to scale than start-ups because the franchise model is geared towards replicating and growing. You already have the blueprint and the operations manual that will support you in scaling.

With franchising, after you've demonstrated your ability and been successful, you're much more likely to get a good deal on your next franchise or licence and the franchisor will be much more likely to support you to scale.

Carl Reader is a friend of mine who has worked with franchises for a long time. His first piece of advice for any franchisee looking to scale is to maintain the management team. So often, new franchisees enter an agreement with a strong business plan and have the motivation to do well, but once they've secured financing and got started, they allow the business to come to them instead of being managers. Even as a franchisee, you have to find new customers and keep your existing customers. No one else is going to do that for you. You need to maintain the management team and also the management of the business. You're ultimately in control and accountable.

Carl also says that franchisees should work with the system. Over time, franchisees can become disillusioned and expend too much energy complaining about what should or shouldn't be changed rather than working with the model. This is a mistake because the system has been tried and tested, so if you change it, you're not going to be as successful.

Provided you've done your due diligence at the outset, you should focus on making the most out of what you've been given, not trying new, untested ways of doing things. As I've said many times, it's all about finding the things that bring success and repeating them. With a franchise, you already know what will bring you success.

A final note on scaling franchises. Erik Van Horn said that you've got two choices. You can stick to the same service, the same vertical, trying out a slightly different area but one that's close by. Doing the same thing again, essentially. Erik emphasises the idea of the 10,000 kicks is better than a few hundred and then switching and trying something new. Erik believed in having a strong focus and that repetition is key to success.

The other option is to diversify and take on a completely different franchise (eg taking on a dog-care business when you're already running a cleaning business).

My take on the different methods of whether you should stick to one and maximise it completely or to diversify, again depends on your skills. In all businesses there are mostly the same principles in execution, marketing and sales. If it has the same clients, you have a match. If it's completely different, like the roofing and dog care, there are two different client types and how you talk to them is different, so it's not easy to jump from one to the other. The wider you spread your net, the less focus you have, so it really depends on how well your operations are set up. You can always go back to the wheel when growing each of them, but the psychology of the clients and the physiology of your team will allow you find out which works best for you; some prefer doing the same thing over and over again, while others want to do something new thing every day.

Build the software

One of the reasons why we were able to scale so successfully at Fantastic Services was that we didn't just build a strong franchise – we also invested in the software we needed. We looked at the industry and found that what we needed to do would require about thirty new software systems, so we decided to build the software and have it as an asset. This became ServiceOS.com

We found that the best way of doing things was to integrate everything from booking to payments within the same system. This was one of our key strengths – understanding how software can automate processes and then investing in the software to create an asset. Software can make or break your business and we always say, 'technology where we can and people where it matters'. This has, for a long time, been our reason for success. You should be able to rely on both parts for success, however I can't emphasise how important it is to get a system that has the features that maximise and optimise your company, from the booking form to invoicing and payment.

You get wealthy by compounding

If you grow something by 7% year-on-year, in a decade, you'll have nearly doubled your business. That's what compounding does. It has a big impact down the line.

It's important to look at growth over time and strive for it every year, even if it's only a small amount. Remember that repetition is key. Repeat all the things that work in order to build your business.

In many ways, franchising is the definition of compounding because everything is set up to enable you to repeat your success and grow your business year-on-year.

Know your strengths and focus on them

To truly find success, you have to understand what your strengths are and maximise them. You have to ignore the distractions and focus only on the things that will grow your business.

If you focus on your weaknesses and try to improve them, you're probably going to have limited success. Conversely, if you focus on your strengths and find ways to improve them, you'll do much better. The smart business owners put energy into their strengths and hire people to help them with the things they're weak at.

If you do this, you'll end up with a business where everyone is working to their strengths and working well together. When you're good at helping people work well together, maximising is easy.

TOP TIPS FOR MAXIMISING

1. **Reinvest 80% of your profits**. If you take too much of the profits out, or don't get investment from outside, then it's very tempting to plateau. We could easily have plateaued in the third year, as we suddenly were making profits larger than our previous salaries and expectations.

2. **Don't build a house of cards**. Set strong foundations for your business by investing in the right things and hiring the right people from the start. Build assets.

3. **Understand your Wheel of Growth**. Get it to run faster and bigger. You have to go through each step and find what can I do faster or more efficient, step-by-step

4. **Repeat. Repeat. Repeat**. As creative entrepreneurs get bored quickly, it's important to remind yourself to repeat the successes. Always look for new things and new inventions; when something is working, repeat it and scale it.

5. **Whatever your end goal is, have fun in the process**. If your goal is multi-million profits, then it's ok; if your goal or purpose is to make the company that is the best for the planet then do that; it's important to not lose track of what's really important and that this is your life and your decisions, you are the architect of this.

THINK BIG

Set yourself a big goal, eg to own, but not operate, ten companies in ten years. Setting big hairy audacious goals will make you more likely to achieve success in the long-term. Setting SMART goals, Specific, Measured, Achievable, Realistic and Timely goals will help you in the short-term, but goals without a plan are really just dreams.

Summary

When you put the right practices in place from the start and reinvest your profits back into the business, maximising is straightforward. You need to be honest with yourself, though. It might not be possible or the right time to scale.

Conclusion

The key understanding that I want you to take from this book is that almost every single function within your business will have an area that you can grow. My hope is that this book has helped you to identify which areas of your business are worth growing and what you need to do to grow them.

We started talking about franchise as a partnership and the benefits of working together, and how this can create synergy. I moved on to describe how to start a franchise or become a franchisee, by following simple steps, and what to look out for.

I then got into why you need to master marketing. You always need to start with marketing because it's key to the success of the business. Business is about getting the customers and keeping them. Quite simply, if you're not doing the marketing right, you're not going to have a business.

Then we looked at accountability. When you're running a business, you need to make yourself accountable, otherwise you won't be able to grow. Sales and simplicity are also vital to the success of a business because there's no business without sales and when you make things simpler, it's easier to scale.

Your purpose is what motivates you. It's what makes people stay in business, even when things aren't going the right way. At Fantastic Services, we discovered that the welfare of the planet was our purpose. It's directed all our business decisions. We went from being a cleaning company to a cleaning, maintenance and repairs company because our purpose involves sustainability. It's this purpose that will drive us through the next decades. We need to move away from the throwaway, quick-fix culture if we are to have a planet for our children.

Because of the success we've had with Fantastic Services, we've had many opportunities to promote different types of products and businesses, but we've decided against associating with harmful industries or products because they don't fit with our purpose. In the near future, we'll add more sustainable services. We believe that we are the company that can deliver real impact in this area.

The most important lesson that I learned as an entrepreneur is to repeat the things that work. When something is making you money, keep doing it. It's easy to get distracted and come up with new ideas, to constantly try to innovate, but the important thing is to keep repeating the things that you know work.

The world today requires you to be extremely structured, especially if you're scaling, and that's why it's important to systemise. When we started Fantastic Services, we had to build the software ourselves and it took a long time and cost a lot of money. Without systems, and without being systematic, you'll never achieve the synergies of scale which result in real business success.

Every single unit, every single part of your business, has room for optimisation. Do what you need to do to make sure that you optimise in the right way for growth.

Happiness, hard work and health will take you to the next level in your business and your life. Without these things, you won't be able to achieve everything that you're capable of. You need to define success for yourself.

Of course there will be times when things get difficult. In the last decade alone there have been a number of events that have hit us hard financially, and there will continue to be. That's why it's so important to keep the balance and make sure that you prioritise your health and happiness.

Finally, we looked at maximising. When your business is running and the units are working, that's when you've got to maximise to get into growth and scale.

It's the blending of all these fundamental principles that we've discussed that will result in business success. I hope that this book becomes a guiding light in your business.

Contact us

To book any service visit Fantastic Services (fantasticservices.com).

To learn more about franchising and opportunities visit Fantastic Franchise (fantasticfranchise.com).

To learn more about systems and automation, visit ServiceOS (serviceos.com).

I'm active on LinkedIn, so feel free to follow me on linkedin.com/in/runelondon

Join us and follow our mission to create a better planet; follow us on Instagram (@fantasticservices) or Twitter @fantastic as we continue to help and grow locally owned franchisees who support local economies.

Acknowledgements

I wish to thank my father, who has always been a fantastic dad and mentor. My wife and son for giving me time to write this book. My business partner, Anton Skarlatov, for creating this fantastic company with me, and every employee, adviser, consultant, friend, our franchisees and importantly the day-to-day heroes, the Fantastic professionals, who wear the Fantastic Services badge of honour and carry out the work on a daily basis, helping our stakeholders have better, cleaner and safer homes.

During the process of writing this book, through interviews with numerous CEOs in franchising and successful franchisees, I have also gained many new friends and peers who will continue to inspire and to be sources of inspiration.

The Author

Rune Sovndahl is co-founder of FantasticServices.com – a leading domestic service franchise, delivering more than fifty home services and operating on four continents.

Born in Copenhagen, Denmark, Rune co-founded Fantastic Services in 2008 with just £3,000 investment and has grown the company to a multimillion-pound network in little over a decade. Using innovative technologies, combined with a sustainable philosophy and constant reinvestment in his work force, Rune harbours a passionate drive that there is a better way to do Fantastic Business.

Rune holds a BA(Hons) in Business Administration and twenty years in the school of 'being in business'. He is a father and has adventure sports as hobbies, having successfully launched the most popular dive shop in Tulum, Mexico – see Instagram @kooxadventures for his hobby business.

Feel free to contact Rune for advice. Drop him a note; let's be inspired!

🌐 www.fantasticbusiness.com
in www.linkedin.com/in/runelondon
✉ rune@sovndahl.dk

Lightning Source UK Ltd.
Milton Keynes UK
UKHW021100050822
406888UK00011B/195